HAL LEONARD
BASS METHOD

MUSIC THEORY

BY SEAN MALONE

PLAYBACK+

Speed • Pitch • Balance • Loop

To access audio visit:
www.halleonard.com/mylibrary

4678-1978-3376-0632

ISBN 978-0-634-05715-1

HAL•LEONARD®

7777 W. BLUEMOUND RD. P.O. BOX 13819 MILWAUKEE, WI 53213

In Australia Contact:
Hal Leonard Australia Pty. Ltd.
4 Lentara Court
Cheltenham, Victoria, 3192 Australia
Email: ausadmin@halleonard.com

Visit Hal Leonard Online at **www.halleonard.com**

PRÉLUDE

How would you define the word "music?" That's a question I can gladly say won't be answered in this book, but I'm going to ask it nonetheless. As the cliché goes, for every question about music we answer, two more appear; music demands to be understood but so grudgingly reveals its secrets. Music is part mathematics, psychology, aesthetics, philosophy, and physics—any one of which could take volumes to explain.

Frequently, the word "music" is used as a metaphor, as in "The crying of my newborn son is music to my ears." We sometimes use the word "music" to elevate: "She recited the poem as if it were music." The late pianist Glenn Gould once defined music as "Man's protection against the arbitrary." There seems to be a common thread running through all of those colorful examples, but it would be difficult to pin it down.

We could take a scientific approach and define music as "wavelengths of sound that are pleasing to the ear." A more artistic approach would be to describe music as "beauty in the form of sound," but as we all know, there are works of "art" called music that have little to do with beauty and only a marginal relationship with sound. Here is a comparatively neutral and practical definition for music: "The purposeful organization of pitch through time." The basic idea is that we're dealing with pitches, they are organized and experienced through time, and this organization is in some way purposeful. I'd be willing to bet you may be thinking of some music that resists this definition, and you may very well be correct. My point in offering a definition—as general as it is—serves as a starting place and provides some basic boundaries. So, I'm not trying to *exclude* the music that may fall out of bounds, instead, we're consciously choosing the materials with which we will construct and organize music so that we may be able to deal with *any* kind of music on its own terms.

WHY DO YOU WANT TO LEARN MUSIC THEORY?

This question may be the most important one to ask, even though it's probably the one least raised. Having goals in mind is essential for your study of music theory as the means of measuring your progress. However, measuring your improvement in "knowing about music" can be as difficult as evaluating your progress in "how to write poems." Without some idea of how these concepts apply to the music you are playing and writing, learning music theory can become a bottomless pit of frustration. So, why do you want to learn music theory? So that you can learn to sightread? So you can write your own music in standard notation? So you can learn how to improvise? Any one of these would be a good reason, but even if you can't yet explain why, your curiosity alone is reason enough to continue.

DO WE NEED TO STUDY MUSIC THEORY?

The codifying of music into theory took hundreds of years to standardize, and it continues to evolve today. By design, theory follows practice; as a new manner of composing emerges, a theory to explain (and ultimately teach) it becomes necessary. Whether or not we learn how to play "by the book" we nonetheless develop our own code in order for music to make sense to us. For example, did someone show you how to play a scale before you learned what the note names were or how the scale is constructed? If so, by memorizing the pattern you played on the fingerboard you created your own code for "scale"; the music theory found in this book is simply the code most musicians use to speak to one another.

If you already have some playing experience, then learning music theory becomes a process of mapping your own code (whether it's explicit or subconscious) onto the standards and conventions kept between musicians today. Why is this distinction important? Because a great deal of what you'll be learning won't be new to you at all. Instead, you'll be learning to translate your unique version of the musical experience into the common language spoken by all musicians today. In other words, trust your musical instincts and be introspective about the learning process. By asking yourself how you may "know" one concept that seems clear to you will aid you invaluably when you're tackling a concept that is giving you some difficulty.

INTRODUCTION

Music Theory for Bassists is a resource for those interested in expanding their knowledge of the vocabulary and grammar of music. As a bassist, I have noticed through performing, composing, and teaching that seeing and hearing things "from the bottom-up" offers certain advantages: distinguishing chord changes, locking in with the drummer, and providing support for melody, to name but a few. Bass, either electric or acoustic, plays a pivotal role in any ensemble: bass supports and influences the harmony, provides a rhythmic motor, can share melodic duties, and has a vast sonic palette. Music theory then becomes an especially powerful tool for a bassist, preparing you for professional opportunities and deepening your personal appreciation of music.

This book serves as a bridge between your experience as a bass player (beginner and pro alike) and the world of musicians who speak this common language; it's a kind of codebook that translates *your* private language into the common tongue.

HOW TO USE THIS BOOK

This book is a compromise between the fundamentals of music theory and how they relate to the bass. I say it's a compromise because there are many topics you would find in a college theory course absent in this book simply because they don't immediately apply directly to the instrument. Accordingly, this book is not meant to be an exhaustive music theory text; rather, it's meant to be an *applied* theory text rendered through the eyes and ears of a bassist. And as such, it will complement any additional method book(s) you may already be using.

This book is organized in such a way that one needn't start from the beginning in order to understand subsequent chapters. So long as you feel comfortable with each chapter, you can dive into whatever topic interests you. However, there is a caveat: unless you are proficient with each concept, some of the concepts that follow simply won't make sense. Even if you are familiar with, say, scales and modes, be sure that all of the material makes sense to you before you move on to chords. This will save you untold frustration—the main reason people abandon the study of music theory.

I have to admit that the best way to learn music theory is in a classroom environment, or at least person-to-person. Nothing beats the interaction between student and teacher; this allows for the student to ask questions and the teacher to adjust for student learning styles. Some students are more visually driven, others aurally, so this book also contains companion audio tracks to help accommodate everyone. Where you see the audio icon followed by a number, this represents the track number for each example. Some examples are played without the bass part so that you can play along. It's not *impossible* to learn theory from a book, but it takes dedication and discipline similar to that which you bring to your instrument. Therefore, this book is presented as a combination theory text/private lesson. The writing is, for the most part, in a style consistent with a conversation rather than endless lists of rules, tables, bullet points, and figures (though there are plenty of those too). I attempt to address common questions and provide bassist-oriented solutions. Think of music theory as an instrument—one that has to be practiced daily just like your bass playing. But how do you "practice" theory?

If you were learning a foreign language, you would try to speak, write, and think in that language throughout the day. Musically speaking, try to apply whatever concepts you are studying to the music you're playing: try to determine the keys, scales, and modes you're using. If you're learning the melody to a tune, determine the intervals found in the melody and how they would transpose to another key—this could be the basis for a solo, for example. Part of your goal should be to begin describing your musical environment with the tools and terminology you will be learning in this book. Above all, each theoretical concept should be represented in *sound*; otherwise music is only graphic art.

Try to pace yourself through each chapter. It takes time for theory to take root and reveal itself in the music you're playing. If you find yourself getting frustrated, take a break until you feel ready and energized to dive back in again. Try to establish a routine, much like your practice routine, and set aside certain times each week to work through this book. Try to find someone who is willing to partner with you, or who may already have studied music theory. It's suggested that three times a week, about an hour each time would be a good pace—it's one similar to a college theory course. But don't worry about the finish line; a steady, consistent stride is all you'll need.

You should give yourself a pat on the back for taking on this challenge—to learn the materials of music. It's not an easy task, but neither is learning how to play an instrument. Yes, there will be times when you will want to permanently close this book out of frustration. During those times, what you have to keep in mind is that the reward is worth the effort. Just as you practice the same patterns on your fingerboard over and over again, you do so because you basically believe it's contributing to your improvement. The same is true of music theory, no matter how technical or dry it may seem at times; when the light bulb turns on—*and it will*—you'll never perform, compose, or listen to music the same way again.

Most of all, take your time, and enjoy the book. Learning music theory can greatly intensify how you already feel about music, as well as help reveal to you the language of musical style and improvisation—something invaluable for a rewarding career as a bassist, performer, and composer.

Sean Malone
Tallahassee, Florida
www.seanmalone.net

ACKNOWLEDGMENTS

Thanks to: the Hal Leonard team for all of their help and patience; Tony, John, Michael, Emmett, and Jim for their generosity; Anthony Corona at DR Strings and Matt Pickford at Ampeg; Andreas and Matthias at Toontrack; and to my students and colleagues who provided feedback and insight each step of the way.

Additional books by the same author published by Hal Leonard:

Dictionary of Bass Grooves (HL00695266)
A Portrait of Jaco: The Solos Collection (HL00660114)
Rock Bass (HL00695801)

Links:

ampeg.com   drstrings.com
johnmyung.com   manthing.com
stick.com   tonylevin.com
toontrack.com

CHAPTER 1: PROPERTIES OF SOUND

Before we discuss the grammar of "pitches purposefully organized through time," it's important to have a basic understanding of sound itself. Whether you play electric or acoustic bass, what they both have in common are vibrating strings—and that's where our story begins.

WAVES

Sound is generated by objects that vibrate, and those vibrations move through the air as *waves*—just like waves in the ocean. Sound waves radiate outward from their source, and their energy is *attenuated* (lessened) over time. Everything from relative humidity to the shape of the room affects the rate of attenuation. Have you ever found the perfect equalizer (e.q.) setting for your bass in your rehearsal space, then when you set up at a gig with same exact e.q. it all of a sudden sounds different? It's not your amp or your bass; it's the *room* that sounds different.

A sound wave has several properties. As it is first pushed through the air a *crest* of increased air density is created, and as the molecules pull apart, a *trough* is created. A *cycle* is the period of time between two adjacent crests; we call this a sound wave's *frequency,* and it is expressed as cycles per second, or *Hertz* (Hz).

Frequency is what we perceive and interpret as *pitch*. For example, a well-known frequency is 440Hz—meaning 440 crests pass in the time of one second; this is the pitch A, the one you hear when an orchestra tunes. We also refer to the distance between crests as the *wavelength*. A pitch sounds "higher" when the wavelength is shorter, and a pitch sounds "lower" when the wavelength is longer.

When we compare the difference in density between the crest (more dense) and the trough (less dense) we are determining the *amplitude*, which we perceive and interpret as *volume* (loudness and softness). A pitch is produced only when a wave propagates in a regular fashion, meaning that no matter how complex the wave, it still has repeating pattern; this is called a *periodic* wave. A wave that is irregular is said to be *aperiodic*, and is considered to be noise.

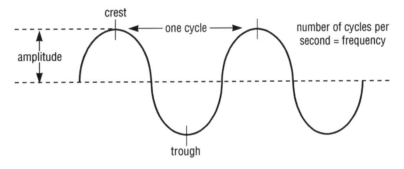

All of these properties are converted into electrical impulses through the magnetic pickups of the bass (or a microphone on an acoustic bass), sent through an amplifier, then converted back into sound by a speaker at a much higher amplitude.

TIMBRE

Every wave, whether complex or simple, has at its foundation a frequency called the *fundamental*. Above the fundamental are a series of frequencies that are whole-number multiples of the fundamental in ever-decreasing amplitude. These frequencies are called *harmonics* (or *partials*), and everything together is called the *overtone series*. This means that when you pluck your E string and let it ring, you are not only hearing the pitch E, but also the overtones generated above it.

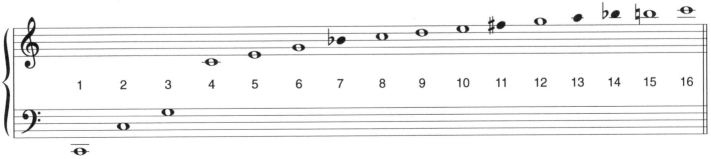

5

Don't be too concerned with the names of all the pitches in the series for the time being. The main points to take from this are 1) the notes you play on your instrument are actually comprised of many pitches, and 2) that the overtone series is the starting place for Western music theory.

An instrument's unique sonic character (or *tone color*) is referred to as its *timbre* (pronounced TAM-bur). For instance, if a flute, guitar, and piano all played a B♭, the timbre is how we'd be able to identify each instrument since they're all playing the same note. Timbre is affected by the method in which the vibration is generated, as well as the materials of which the instrument is made. For example, a plucked note on an electric bass compared to a bowed note on an acoustic bass.

QUESTIONS FOR REVIEW

1. How is sound created?
2. What are *waves*?
3. Define *frequency, pitch, wavelength, amplitude,* and *periodic.*
4. What is the *overtone series*?
5. What is *timbre*?

TOPICS FOR FURTHER STUDY

1. The envelope of sound: attack, sustain, and release
2. Constructive and destructive interference between sound waves
3. "Harmonic nodes" and where they are found on the bass
4. Reading: *On the Sensations of Tone* by Hermann Helmholtz

CHAPTER 2: FUNDAMENTALS

STEPS AND LEAPS

Perhaps the most basic unit of music is *pitch*—a tone that is described as being either high or low, and is defined by its frequency. The musical "space" between pitches, or the distance a pitch moves, is measured by *step* or by *leap*. A *half* step is the distance of one fret on the fingerboard (on the same string), and a *whole* step is two frets. A *leap* is anything larger than a whole step.

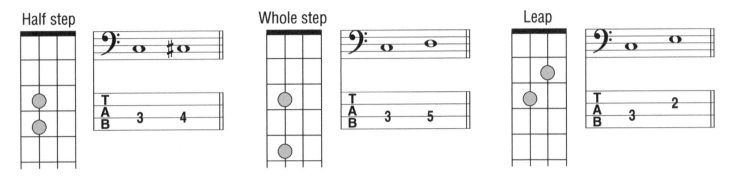

THE MUSICAL ALPHABET

Western music utilizes the first seven letters of the alphabet to represent the seven basic pitch names: A–B–C–D–E–F–G, each of which corresponds to a particular frequency of sound. Each time the musical alphabet repeats, it is said that we encounter a new *octave* (*octa* being the prefix for *eight*). Numbers are used after the note name to indicate the octave register.

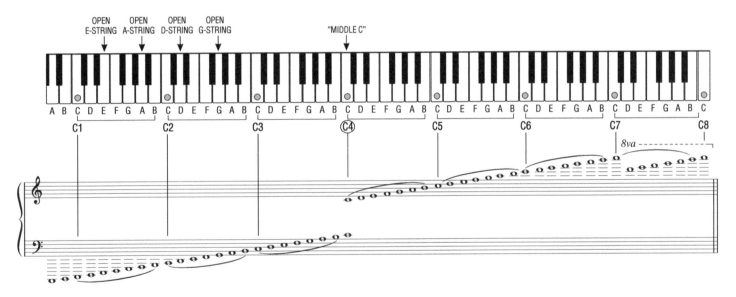

For example, pitches A4 up to (but not including) A5, are said to belong to the same *octave register*. We can think of the pitch A5 as an octave higher than A4—it's the "same" pitch, only higher.

MUSIC NOTATION

Western music notation is written from left to right on a *staff* (plural *staves*) consisting of five lines and four spaces.

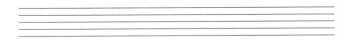

The horizontal dimension of the staff represents the passage of time. The vertical dimension of the staff represents difference in pitch. The *range* of the staff—the high and low boundary of pitch frequency—is indicated by a *clef*, a symbol placed at the beginning of the staff. There are several kinds of clefs, each with a different range, and music for the bass is written in the *bass clef.*

The bass clef has two dots above and below the fourth line, which is the pitch F. Because of this, the bass clef is sometimes called the F clef, and older versions of this clef actually looked like a capital cursive F. Vertical lines on the staff are called *bar lines* and they separate *measures* (also called *bars*). Two thin vertical lines make a *double bar line* (mostly used at the end of a section) and a thick line preceded by a thin line is a *final bar line*, used to indicate the end of the piece.

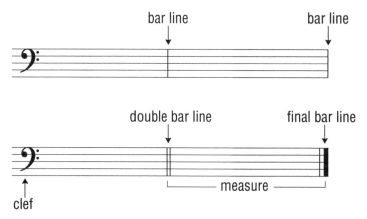

NOTES ON THE STAFF

The letter name of a note is determined by its location on the lines and spaces of the staff. The lines of the staff are (from low to high) G–B–D–F–A, and the spaces are A–C–E–G. For the lines you can say: "**G**ood **B**assists **D**o **F**ine **A**lways." For the spaces you can say: "**A**ll **C**ows **E**at **G**rass," or make up your own acronym. Either way, it's crucial to learn the notes of the staff as quickly as possible.

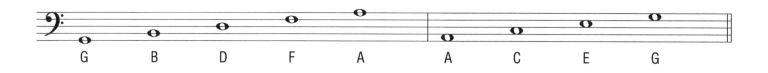

| G | B | D | F | A | A | C | E | G |

Though we're concentrating on the bass clef, it is important to know the other clefs in use today. Here are the clefs, their names, and their ranges:

| Treble | Bass | Alto | Tenor | Middle C (C4) in each clef |

| G | F | C | C |

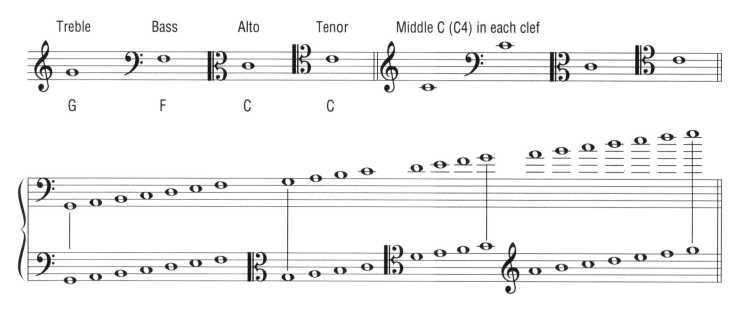

Sometimes the treble clef and the bass clef are linked together; this is called a *grand staff* and is most often used for piano music.

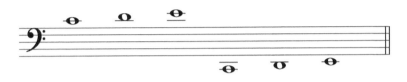

If pitches exceed the range of the staff, *ledger lines* are used to provide a place to notate them.

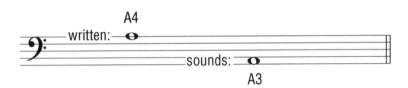

It is important to note early on that the bass is a *transposing* instrument: the notes written on the staff aren't the pitches we hear when they are played. Bass transposes an octave lower than written. If an A4 is written (top line) and played, the sound we hear is A3, an octave below it (the first space). The reason for this is to keep the notation simple. If the pitches were written as they sound, they would be many ledger lines below the staff, making them difficult to read.

You may want to write a passage that exceeds the staff but are concerned there will be too many ledger lines to read. To solve this problem, the passage can be written either an octave higher or lower than desired, with an *ottava* sign to indicate the preferred octave.

When the pitches should be played an octave *higher* than written, the symbol *8va* (*ottava*) followed by a dashed line is written over the desired notes. When the pitches should be played an octave *lower* than written, the symbol *8vb* (ottava *bassa*) followed by a dashed line is written beneath the notes. You won't see this in most bass parts, because as we noted, all bass parts sound an octave lower than written. However, you will probably encounter music written for other instruments, so you should know what *8vb* means.

When the passage should return to the original octave register as written, the word *loco* (Italian for *at place*) is written over that pitch. A third symbol, called a *quindicesima* (written *15ma*), means the part should be performed two octaves higher than written, but this is rarely seen by the bassist.

ACCIDENTALS

Accidentals are symbols placed to the left of a notehead that raise or lower pitches by a specific distance. For every pitch, the following accidentals can apply:

1. ♯ Sharp: raises the pitch one half step.

2. ♭ Flat: lowers the pitch one half step.

3. ♮ Natural: cancels previous accidentals.

4. 𝄪 Double sharp: raises the pitch one whole step.

5. ♭♭ Double flat: lowers the pitch one whole step.

ENHARMONIC SPELLING

If the note C is raised by one half step, it becomes a C♯. If the pitch D is lowered one half step, it becomes a D♭. This means that the pitches C♯ and D♭ actually sound the same, though they have different letter names. Pitches that have different letter names but sound the same are called *enharmonic* pitches. In fact, most notes have up to three letter names. Below is a chart of the bass neck representing all of the notes available on the fingerboard. When there are two notes in a fret, that means the pitch has two enharmonic names.

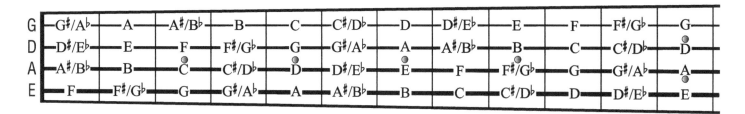

The following are examples of enharmonic equivalence:

But why do notes have more than one name? We haven't gotten far enough just yet for a full explanation. Instead here is an analogy: in the English language there are words that *sound* the same but *mean* something different; they're called *homonyms*. The reason we choose one or the other has to do with which word makes sense in a sentence. As we'll see later, pitch names must be "spelled" in a manner that makes sense in context: C♯ *means* something different from D♭, and we'll learn that meaning later on in the book.

When an accidental occurs, it applies to all subsequent occurrences of that note within the same measure unless otherwise indicated, though not necessarily in different octaves. For example, if a sharp is placed next to the pitch C4 it becomes C♯4, and unless otherwise noted, every other C (such as C3) is still a C♮. The very next bar line cancels out any added accidentals, though a composer may include a *courtesy accidental* in parentheses to remind the performer that the pitch has changed back.

With the use of accidentals, an octave can be divided into twelve half steps. The first example illustrates the use of sharps and the second example illustrates the use of flats. The "tab" staff underneath is bass tablature.

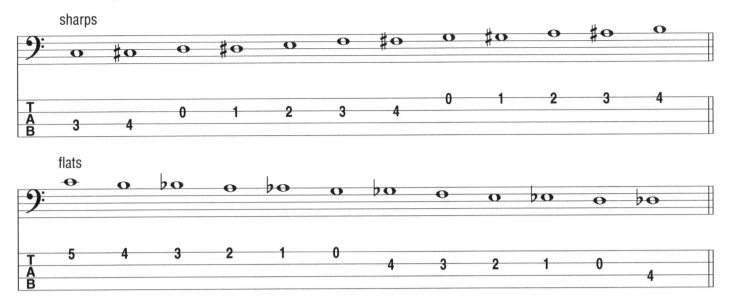

When should you use a sharp instead of a flat, or vice versa? The rule of thumb is: if the overall direction of the music is ascending, use a sharp. If the overall direction of the music is descending, use a flat.

As you will see, there is an exception for just about every "rule." Whenever you need to make a choice—and this goes for *everything* concerning notation—choose the simplest and clearest way possible to communicate your idea, even if it might break the "rules."

The symbols that occur at the beginning of the staff, the key signature and the *time* (or *meter*) *signature*, may change at any place during the course of the composition. If the new key or meter begins on the next musical line, called a system, the new signature is written as the last item in the system that precedes it. This gives a warning to the performer that the change is coming.

NOTE AND REST VALUES

Notes consist of a *notehead* (either filled-in or open), and may also include a *stem*, one or more *flags*, and a *dot* next to the notehead.

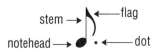

The number of flags, the presence of a dot, and whether the notehead is filled in all determine a note's duration, or *value*. The following chart illustrates each note type and its value in relation to the others:

NAME	VALUE				
Breve (double whole)	𝅘𝅥	=	o	+	o
Whole	o	=	𝅗𝅥	+	𝅗𝅥
Half	𝅗𝅥	=	♩	+	♩
Quarter	♩	=	♪	+	♪
Eighth	♪	=	𝅘𝅥𝅯	+	𝅘𝅥𝅯
Sixteenth	𝅘𝅥𝅯	=	𝅘𝅥𝅰	+	𝅘𝅥𝅰
Thirty-second	𝅘𝅥𝅰	=	𝅘𝅥𝅱	+	𝅘𝅥𝅱
Sixty-fourth	𝅘𝅥𝅱				

Note values are expressed as simple fractions. Beginning with the whole note as 1, a half note is ½ the value of a whole note, a quarter note is ¼ the value of a whole note, and an eighth note is ⅛ the value of a whole note, etc. This means that one whole note is worth two half notes, or four quarter notes, or eight eighth notes, and so on. Every time the bottom note of the fraction doubles, it represents half the value.

RESTS

A *rest* tells the performer that there should be silence for a specified amount of time. For every note, there is a symbol that represents the same value in terms of silence. Here are the types of rests and their corresponding values:

NAME	VALUE				
Breve (double whole)	▪	=	▬	+	▬
Whole	▬	=	▬	+	▬
Half	▬	=	𝄽	+	𝄽
Quarter	𝄽	=	𝄾	+	𝄾
Eighth	𝄾	=	𝄿	+	𝄿
Sixteenth	𝄿	=	𝅀	+	𝅀
Thirty-second	𝅀	=	𝅁	+	𝅁
Sixty-fourth	𝅁				

DOTS

If you encounter a dot placed to the lower right of a notehead, the duration of the note is increased by one half of its metrical value (a). If a second dot is written, then half the value of the first dot is added (b).

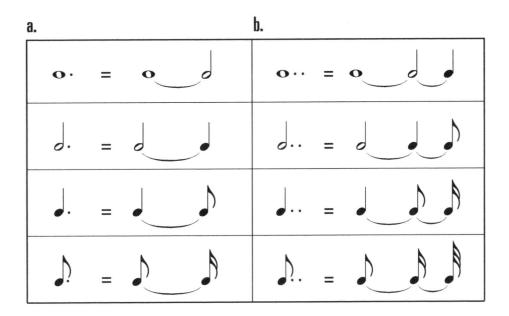

a.   b.

13

NOTE POSITION

Notes and rests should be horizontally positioned in proportion to their value. For example, if a measure equals a whole note, then each quarter note or rest receives one quarter the length of the measure, and two eighth notes or four sixteenth notes should all equally fit in the same space.

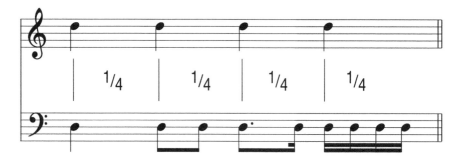

An exception to the placement rule is made with a full-measure rest.

STEM DIRECTION

When dealing with a single staff containing only one musical part (as you would see for any bass part), all of the notes that are written below the center line of the staff (D) should have the stems written to the right of the notehead and point upward. For all of the notes written above the center line, stems are drawn on the left side of the notehead and point downward. If a note is drawn on the center line, the stem can go either up or down depending on the majority of the other stem directions in the measure. The length of a stem should be about one octave.

QUESTIONS FOR REVIEW

1. What is a *staff*?

2. Define an *octave*.

3. What are *ledger lines* used for?

4. What's another name for the pitch A♭♭?

5. What does *enharmonic* mean?

TOPICS FOR FURTHER STUDY

1. Alternative staves and alternate notation

2. Music calligraphy and engraving

3. Any book on handwritten music notation—don't rely on notation software

CHAPTER 3: BASS NOTATION

Articulations are symbols written above the notehead and are explicit instructions on how to perform the note. This chapter deals with a variety of articulations and how they are performed on the bass, as well as how they look in notation and tab. Portions are excerpted from my book *Rock Bass* (Hal Leonard).

Hammer-On

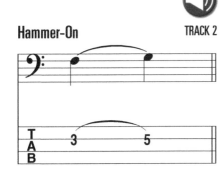

Hammer-On   TRACK 2

The *hammer-on* is performed by picking or striking the first note (the lower note), then on the same string "hammering" the higher note with another finger. The sound of the second note is generated by the impact of the finger that's doing the hammering and the already vibrating string. The effect it creates is one where the second note has a lesser attack and feels more "attached" to the first note. This helps achieve a *legato* (smooth) phrase—one that sounds smoother than if you picked or plucked both of the notes.

The hammer-on is not limited to only two notes; you can pick one and then hammer with as many fingers as you choose, including the other hand, but that gets us into *tapping*, another technique we'll soon see.

Pull-Off

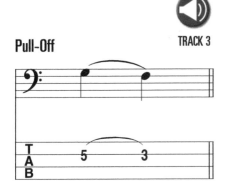

Pull-Off   TRACK 3

The *pull-off* is similar to the hammer-on, but in reverse. Start by fingering a note with either your fourth or third finger, while your first finger is resting on the same string, two or three frets lower. After the note is sounded, pull off your (third or fourth) finger in such a way that it causes the string to vibrate further; the finger that you are pulling off is acting like your picking hand. An excellent way to practice this technique is to focus on the fretting hand alone: try pulling off the note with your third or fourth finger without the benefit of your picking hand. This will build strength, independence, and coordination. As with the hammer-on, the pull-off is a *legato* technique that creates a smooth connection between notes.

Legato Slide

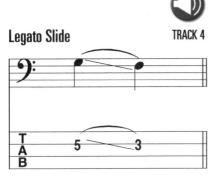

Legato Slide   TRACK 4

The *legato slide* is a slight variation of the hammer-on or pull-off; everything is the same except that you slide using the same finger instead of hammering on or pulling off from another. Also, when you arrive at the second note, it is not struck again, which means you must keep enough pressure on the string so that the note continues to ring after executing the slide.

This technique is useful when you'd like to hear the notes in between the beginning and ending pitches—something that sounds especially nice on a fretless or acoustic bass. You may also choose this technique when you are shifting position or changing fingering; it allows you to get where you need to be while at the same time creating an interesting sound to fill the gap. Slides are often heard on the weak beats of the measure (especially at the end), functioning much in the same way a conjunction does in a sentence; slides connect notes in a subtle and expressive way.

Shift Slide

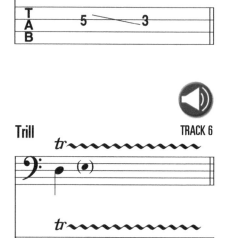

The *shift slide* is identical to the legato slide except that both notes are struck; by striking the second note, its arrival is more punctuated. When the second note occurs on the downbeat of the measure, the shift slide is an effective way of approaching it. A word of caution when performing either slide: be sure to evenly distribute the distance covered on the fingerboard over time, especially when using a fretted bass. The reason for this is that each half-step on a fretted bass is much more pronounced than on a fretless, and if the slide starts off slow then suddenly speeds up, the connection can sound awkward rather than smooth.

Trill

Almost every pitched instrument is capable of producing a *trill*. In the case of bass guitar, a trill is performed by rapidly alternating between notes by hammering on and pulling off the string. Every trill is notated with two notes: the first note is the note being decorated, and the second—usually notated above as a smaller, unstemmed notehead—indicates the interval between the two, often a half or whole step. There is no metric value indicated with a trill, though it is often a subdivision of the beat. A rule of thumb for trills is that they are played rapidly, though comfortably, and should "fit" rhythmically within the pulse of the meter.

The trill is a type of articulation known as an *ornament*, meaning that one note is more "important" than the other (in this case, either belonging to a chord, and/or in a metrically strong position within the measure) and the second note decorates the first. Trills often sound better in the higher register of the instrument.

Tremolo Picking

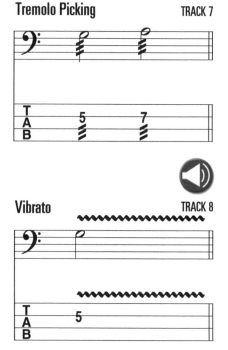

Tremolo picking is the continuous and rapid picking of a note. The most frequent use of this figure occurs at song endings; the final chord is struck and as the drummer is playing fills, the bassist tremolo-picks the root note, until everyone plays the final accent. However this is not the only application of tremolo picking. The notation used—lines through a stemmed note—is a kind of shorthand. Instead of writing all of the notes out, the composer may just use the tremolo picking notation, indicating only what pitches should have a tremolo applied.

Vibrato

The cornerstone of expression is *vibrato*, and it comes in two distinct varieties. The first type is created when the fretting hand bends the string up and down in a motion parallel to the frets. The second type consists of the fretting hand pivoting on a note, rolling back and forth perpendicular to the frets. On the fretted bass, the first type of vibrato is more common; it creates pitches slightly higher than the fretted note when the string is bent and pulled. The second type of vibrato is more common on the fretless bass, creating pitches both above and below the target pitch.

Oftentimes a bassist can overdo vibrato, resulting in a jittery, nervous sound. It only takes a little bit of effort to create a natural sounding vibrato, and listening to other instruments such as the cello, violin, flute, and oboe can give you an excellent model to emulate. Ultimately it comes down to a matter of taste, but by practicing bass alone in a deliberate, conscious manner the subtlety of vibrato becomes more apparent. A good place to start is simply to play scales very slowly, since each finger of the fretting hand gets a turn. Don't neglect the third finger, it's often weak and needs a little more attention to get it sounding like the others.

Shake

The *shake* may be considered a kind of special effect; you can think of it like a vibrato that has gone slightly out of control. One finger on the fretting hand rapidly alternates between two notes, often a half step above or below the target pitch. Applying shake to a note brings attention to it, and it can very quickly become overused. Whereas vibrato could be used on every note, shake should be reserved for special, heavily accented occasions. Similar to vibrato, however, shake should be practiced with each finger of the fretting hand for the sake of maintaining consistency.

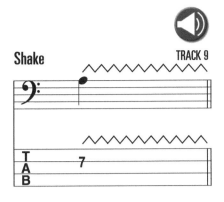

Natural Harmonic

Harmonics have been used mainly as a means of tuning the instrument, at the fifth and seventh frets. There are more natural harmonics all over the fingerboard, and having knowledge of those pitches can add bell-like chimes to your bass lines. The key to playing harmonics is applying just enough pressure to allow the note to ring, but not so much that the string is prevented from vibrating. The fretting hand should be placed right on top of the fret, not in between the frets, both for fretted and fretless basses. The most commonly used natural harmonics are over the twelfth, seventh, fifth, and fourth frets. Natural harmonics found in other locations are a bit more difficult to play and require a delicate touch from the fretting hand. The late, great bassist Jaco Pastorius is credited for realizing the potential of harmonics, evidenced in his composition "Portrait of Tracy" on his first solo album.

Bend

A *bend* is very straightforward: strike a note and bend the string with your fretting hand, causing the pitch to rise. On the staff, bends are notated with a small stemless notehead joined to a regular note with a pointed slur. The tablature indicates the distance between the two notes, most often a half or whole step. The tricky part of a bend is maintaining correct intonation, especially since each string requires a different amount of tension in order to reach the intended pitch. To practice, perform the bend, then play the same pitch without bending to it and compare the two.

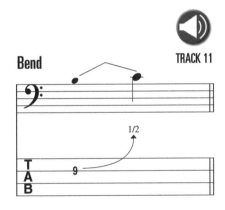

Muffled (Muted) Strings

Muffled, or muted, strings can be played two different ways. First, the fretting hand can lie across the strings, lightly touching them so that they are unable to vibrate when the string is plucked, sounding much like a "thud." The second method is performed by striking a string with one finger of the picking hand and then quickly muting it with a second finger. Muted notes add a percussive element to bass lines and are an integral part of the funk-rock sound. Something to consider is that a muted bass note shares similar frequencies with those of the kick drum and can serve a similar function in the total makeup of the rhythm section. Muffled strings propel the groove, regardless of style, and are the fingerstyle equivalent of the slap and pop technique.

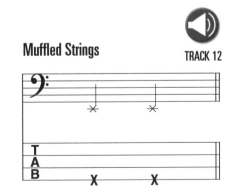

Bend and Release

The *bend and release* is just an elaborated version of a bend; instead of ending on the "bent" note, the bend is released back to the original pitch.

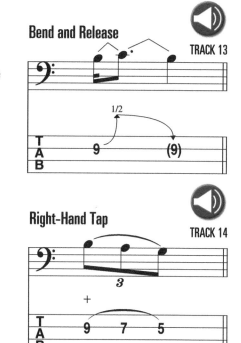

Bend and Release

TRACK 13

Right-Hand Tap

Tapping—either with the left or right hand—is a technique as well as a style of playing. For example, you could play many figures with either a traditional style (picking with one hand and fretting with the other), or by tapping, which produces a different texture and timbre. The most unique feature of tapping is the percussive attack of the notes, created by the fingers acting as a kind of hammer. You can combine many of the items already discussed; for example, you could tap a note with your right hand then bend and release it.

Right-Hand Tap

TRACK 14

Though the terms "left" and "right" are used, these assume that you are right-handed. With that in mind, consider "right" to mean picking hand, and "left" to mean fretting hand. The right-hand tap is done by striking a note on the fretboard with your picking hand, generating enough force to cause the string to vibrate. You could use any number of fingers, though one to three fingers is most common. You're not limited to single notes; you can tap two notes on different strings, as well as triads on three strings.

Left-Hand Tap

The *left-hand tap*, or fretting-hand tap, is identical in technique to the right-hand tap. The object is to strike the string cleanly and forcefully enough to cause the string to vibrate. Any finger or fingers can be used, though you may find the third finger and possibly the fourth are a bit weaker than the first and second. Practicing third and fourth fingers in isolation can improve your technique.

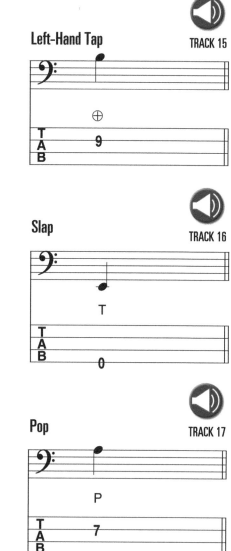

Left-Hand Tap

TRACK 15

Slap

The *slap* technique is performed by the picking hand; the thumb strikes the string approximately in the area of the knuckle, creating a percussive attack. To improve coordination between your thumb technique and your fretting hand, practice playing some simple figures—scales, for example—using only your thumb to generate the sound. Slap technique is essential to funk-rock and generally sounds better when played on a fretted bass due to the metal strings hitting the metal frets.

Slap

TRACK 16

Pop

The *pop* technique is the companion to the slap technique, and is performed by hooking a finger(s) underneath the string(s), pulling upward, and letting go. The sound generated is more aggressive than when the string is plucked in the usual way; it matches the intensity of the slap sound. When you've reached a comfortable level of coordination with your slapping technique, slowly incorporate the pop technique.

Pop

TRACK 17

CHAPTER 4: INTERVALS

An *interval* is the difference in pitch between two notes. When the two notes are played simultaneously, it's called a harmonic interval. When the two notes are played in succession, it's called a melodic interval.

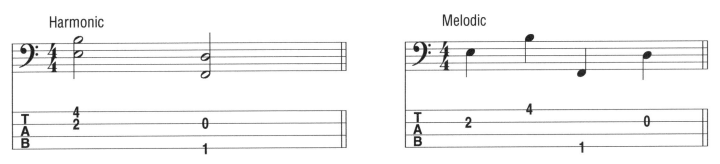

Interval measurements have two parts: *size* and *quality*. There are several ways to determine the size and quality of intervals, and like note names, there are intervals with enharmonic spellings.

INTERVAL SIZE

Also referred to as *quantity*, the size of an interval can be easily determined by how many letters of the alphabet there are from one note to the other. The distances are labelled by number: unison (also called a *prime*), second, third, fourth, fifth, sixth, seventh, and octave. As an example, we'll look at the interval from C up to A.

Starting with the lower note, C, we'll count the number of notes to A, *being sure to always* include both notes of the interval as we count through the musical alphabet.

C	D	E	F	G	A
1	2	3	4	5	6

The distance from C to A is six notes, so it's an interval of a sixth.

Here is another example: F# up to C. When determining the size of an interval, *accidentals do not matter*.

F#	G	A	B	C
1	2	3	4	5

F# up to C is a fifth, and it wouldn't matter if the F was natural or flat, or if the C was sharp, flat, or double flat, etc. As long as it's *some kind* of F up to *some kind* of C, they are still five notes apart, so it is a fifth.

INTERVAL QUALITY

Quality differentiates between intervals of the same (numerical) size. The interval qualities are: major (M), minor (m), diminished (○), augmented (+), and perfect (P). All intervals may be diminished or augmented, though only some are perfect, and the others major or minor. Here is our first set of rules:

Quality: Augmented, Diminished, *Perfect*
Interval: Unisons, Fourths, Fifths, Octaves

Quality: Augmented, Diminished, *Major, Minor*
Interval: Seconds, Thirds, Sixths, Sevenths

Counting half and whole steps, though painstaking, is a reliable method to identify intervals. With experience, you'll find it faster to relate intervals to the major scale, which is discussed extensively in Chapter 5.

On the following page is a chart with intervals and their qualities based on whole and half steps. You'll notice some intervals in italics. Though these are theoretically possible, for the most part they are used rarely (if at all) in practical situations. The rule of thumb is to avoid augmented spellings (except augmented 4ths) whenever possible. It's important to know them all, but the selections in italics are those that you are less likely to see in the "real world." Each entry in italics has a companion interval—its enharmonic equivalent—the more common way to spell that particular interval.

Half Steps	Whole Steps	Notes	Interval Size	Interval Quality	Symbol
0	0	C to C	Unison	Perfect	P1
1	1/2	C to C♯	Unison	Augmented	+1
		C to D♭	Second	Minor	m2
2	1	C to D	Second	Major	M2
3	1 1/2	C to D♯	Second	Augmented	+2
		C to E♭	Third	Minor	m3
4	2	C to E	Third	Major	M3
5	2 1/2	C to E♯	Third	Augmented	+3
		C to F	Fourth	Perfect	P4
6	3	C to F♯	Fourth	Augmented	+4
		C to G♭	Fifth	Diminished	♭5
7	3 1/2	C to G	Fifth	Perfect	P5
8	4	C to G♯	Fifth	Augmented	+5
		C to A♭	Sixth	Minor	m6
9	4 1/2	C to A	Sixth	Major	M6
10	5	C to A♯	Sixth	Augmented *	+6
		C to B♭	Seventh	Minor	m7
11	5 1/2	C to B	Seventh	Major	M7
		C to C♭	Octave	Diminished	♭8
12	6	C to C	Octave	Perfect	P8

*The augmented sixth is rare in pop, jazz, and rock, etc., but is often used in classical music.

Bassist's Solution #1: Determine the Interval by Its Fingerboard Shape

Identifying an interval by its shape on the bass fingerboard is quick, though it may result in misspelling. However, it can be used to quickly narrow things down to a few choices, after which you can apply key or scale theory (coming later) to determine the exact interval. There is more than one way to finger some of these examples, so those covering the smallest number of frets were chosen. Since the bass in tuned in fourths, the shapes stay consistent.

Though the sound and fingering of an interval remains unique and consistent, its spelling may not. For example, the following intervals are all fingered and sound the same:

B–E♯ ⟶ augmented 4th

B–F ⟶ diminished 5th

B–G♭♭ ⟶ doubly-diminished 6th

(The pitches E♯, F, and G♭♭ are all enharmonic.)

Why have so many names for the same sound? As we will see in Chapter 6, it all depends on the key we're in. For now, play these examples on your bass, and be sure to sing them as well:

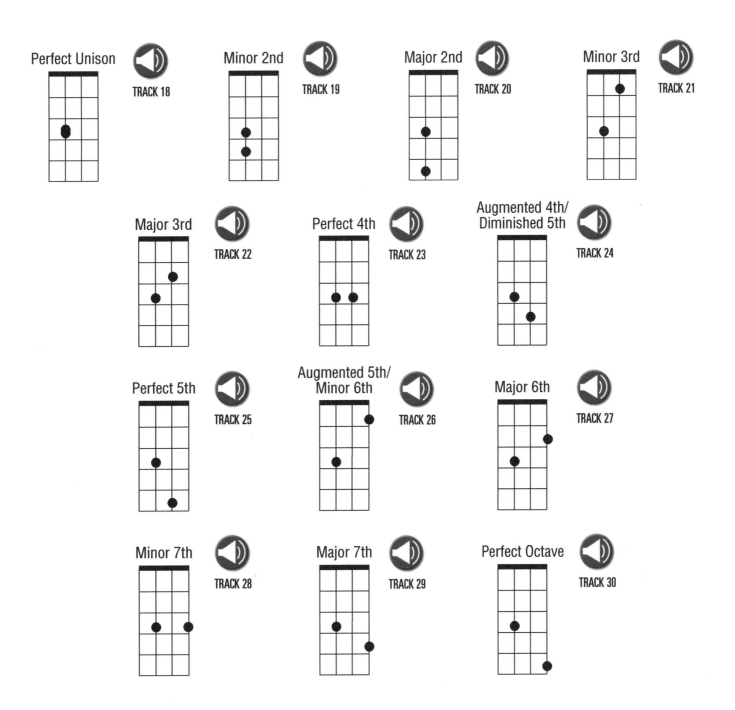

Bassist's Solution #2: Determine the Interval by Its Sound

This solution falls under the heading of ear training, though it is an analogy to Bassist's Solution #1. Each interval has its own unique sound and can therefore be determined by ear. You may have already been introduced to a method of recognizing intervals by using familiar melodies. For example, the first two notes of Wagner's "Bridal Chorus" ("Here Comes the Bride") are a perfect 4th, the theme from the movie *Jaws* prominently features a half step (minor 2nd), and "My Bonnie Lies over the Ocean" begins with a major 6th. Though this method may provide some instant gratification, there is a warning that goes with it as well. The context of the intervals in each melody informs your ability to recognize/memorize them, and if the context (i.e. the harmony) changes, there is a good chance you may not correctly identify the interval.

For example, the first interval of the melody "Here Comes the Bride" is a perfect 4th.

TRACK 31

But if we change the context, all of a sudden it's a little harder to hear "Here Comes the Bride."

TRACK 32

Here is an analogy involving language. Let's say that the word "read" is the sound of our interval in the previous example. Without context, we could pronounce the word "read" either with a long 'e' (like *reed*) or with a short 'e' (like *red*). Now, read the next two sentences out loud:

1. I really want to read this book.

2. Last week I read this book.

In sentence number 1, the *context* is the present tense, so we pronounce it with a long 'e.' Sentence number 2 is in the past tense, so we pronounce it with a short 'e.' In our musical example, when we choose a melody to help us memorize the sound of an interval we are also learning it in *context*. If you place too much importance on the context versus the interval itself, you may be doing more harm than good. Practice playing intervals on your bass and immediately sing each one afterward—this will help associate the visual (notation), with the aural/vocal (singing) and the tactile (fingers on the instrument), reinforcing and informing all the associated skills. When the sound of each interval becomes familiar to you, try playing a note, choose an interval above it and sing it, then play the note to check your accuracy.

ALTERED INTERVALS

As with every concept in this book, we want to develop a reliable and repeatable identification procedure that can be used consistently. It is helpful when learning intervals to determine their size first and their quality second (even though we label intervals the other way around, with the quality first). For example, the following examples are all thirds:

C–E   C#–E   C#–E#   C–E#

Their numeric size remains the same; it's the quality that changes. We can use the following chart to help determine the order to follow for change of quality when the pitch names remain the same:

♭	**1, 4, 5, 8**	↑		♭	**2, 3, 6, 7**	↑
	Augmented				Augmented	
	Perfect				Major	
	Diminished				Minor	
		♯			Diminished	♯

Here are some guidelines for the alterations of intervals:

1. If the same accidental is added to both notes, the quality stays the same.

   C–E or C♯–E♯ or C♭♭–E♭♭: these are all major 3rds.

2. If the bottom note only is *raised*, the interval becomes *smaller*.

3. If the bottom note only is *lowered*, the interval becomes *larger*.

For example, if you have a perfect interval made one half step smaller, it will become *diminished*. If you have a major interval that is made one half step larger, it becomes *augmented*. Let's test this idea with a few examples. The interval from F♯ up to D is a minor 6th. If the bottom note is lowered one half step (F♮–D), the interval becomes larger and is now a major 6th. What if the lower note were raised one half step, and we called it G–D? Is this now a diminished 6th? No. This is no longer some kind of sixth: it's now a fifth because the *note name* has changed. G–D is a perfect 5th. A diminished 6th would be spelled F𝄪–D.

4. If the top note only is raised, the interval becomes *larger*.

5. If the top note only is lowered, the interval becomes *smaller*.

Here is another example: B♭ up to E♭ is a perfect 4th. Raise the top note to E♮ and, by following the chart, we see that the quality changes to augmented. What if we lowered the top note to E♭♭? Is this still some kind of fourth, or is it now some kind of third? (E♭♭ is another name for D.) B♭ up to E♭♭ is a diminished 4th—an interval we rarely (if ever) see, but it is the correct name for this interval nonetheless.

Intervals remain consistent in sound and fingering; only the name changes in context of key. Remember the analogy for enharmonic pitches: two words may sound the same, but they mean something different. Intervals must be spelled a certain way so that their meaning makes sense in terms of the key or chord.

Doubly AUGMENTED	
AUGMENTED	
MAJOR 2, 3, 6, 7	Perfect 1, 4, 5, 8
minor	
diminished	
doubly diminished	

NOTATION OF SECONDS

If an interval or chord contains seconds, then the lower of the two notes is drawn to the left of the stem. Never connect notes that have different metrical values (e.g. a quarter note and a half note) with a single stem.

COMPOUND INTERVALS

So far, all of the intervals we've looked at are all one octave or smaller—referred to as *simple intervals*. When intervals are larger than an octave they're called *compound intervals*, and for a bassist, they are useful tools for harmonization. For any interval whose numerical size is larger than 8 (ninth, tenth, eleventh, twelfth, thirteenth, fourteenth, fifteenth) subtract 7 from the number to arrive at its *simple* equivalent. For example, let's subtract 7 from the compound interval of a ninth. 9 − 7 = 2, so a ninth is a second placed one octave higher.

C3–D3
M2nd

C3–D4
M9th

Simple intervals played harmonically in the low register of the bass can sound very muddy. By using a compound interval, the same quality and effect is achieved while sounding clearer. Here are the unaltered (major and perfect) compound intervals:

Once we get to the fifteenth, another octave of harmonically equivalent intervals starts again: sixteenth, seventeenth, etc. There is no theoretical upper limit to the size of possible intervals. Often when we talk about compound intervals, we refer to them in their simple form as a convenience, then just finger the note an octave higher. This is preferred to memorizing another set of interval sizes and qualities: all compound interval qualities are identical to their simple interval counterparts. By far, the most commonly used compound interval on bass is the tenth, since it is easy to finger and a third above any note is a common harmonization.

Here is a C major scale played with tenths:

TRACK 33

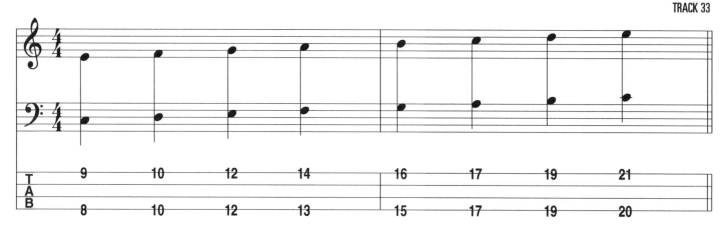

INVERSION

Every interval has a companion: a complementary interval with which it completes an octave. B up to E is a perfect 4th, and E up to B is a perfect 5th; each interval is considered an *inversion* of the other. The word "invert" roughly means to reverse an arrangement, or change something to its opposite; when an interval is inverted the pitches exchange places. You can either place the lower note an octave higher, over the top note (as shown by the arrow in the figure below), or place the higher note an octave lower, below the lower note.

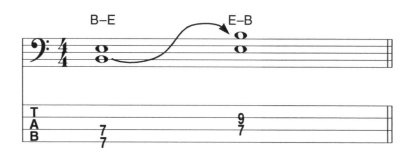

THE RULE OF NINE

To determine the correct size of the inverted interval, subtract the size of the original interval from nine. For example, the inversion of a fourth: 9 – 4 = 5; the inversion of a fourth is a fifth. Similarly, a sixth inverts to a third, a second to a seventh, and a unison to an octave (and all vice versa). Notice that an interval added to its inversion always adds up to nine.

INVERSION AND QUALITY

Just as with interval size, interval quality follows a pattern as well. When inverted, intervals that are:

- perfect remain perfect.
- major invert to minor.
- minor invert to major.
- augmented invert to diminished.
- diminished invert to augmented.

Putting it together then, let's determine the inversion of a major 3rd. Using the rule of nine, the size is a sixth (9 – 3 = 6), and using the chart above, major inverts to minor: the inversion of a major 3rd is a minor 6th. The chart below illustrates common intervals and their inversions; the first note to the second note is the interval, and the second note to the third note is its inversion:

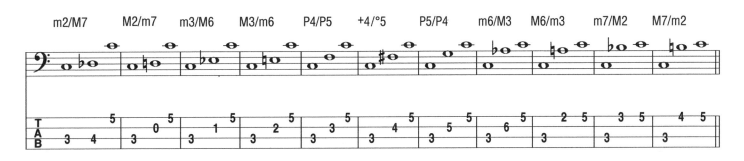

QUESTIONS FOR REVIEW

1. What is *inversion* and why is it important to understand?
2. What is the difference between *simple* and *compound intervals*?
3. What is the *rule of nine*?
4. Why is there more than one name for a single *interval*?
5. Name two kinds of intervals that are rarely seen in the "real world."

TOPICS FOR FURTHER STUDY

1. Paul Hindemith's theory of intervals
2. Play a small section of one of your favorite bass lines. Write out the line as a series of intervals. For example: M2↑ m2↓ m2↑ P5, etc.
3. Play each interval on your bass and think of a word that describes each sound (e.g., a minor second sounds "tense").

CHAPTER 5: SCALE AND MODE—PART I

The concepts of *scale*, *mode*, and *key* are intertwined, and to learn one is to learn the other. However, when first studying them their connection may not be obvious. Knowing only their particular constructions gets us no closer to our goal—to better understand how music *works*—so it's important to pay attention to what scale, mode, and key *do*, and what role they play in defining tonal music.

It seems like everybody knows what a scale is, but how would you define it? The concept of scale has several characteristics, though it is difficult to place them all neatly in one complete sentence, owing to the diversity of scales available. Instead, let's list the characteristics that occur more often than not:

1. A scale is a consecutive, step-wise series of pitches, each with a different letter name in alphabetical order.
2. Scales divide one octave and can both ascend and descend on the staff.
3. A scale organized by a specific order of half and whole steps is referred to as a *diatonic collection*.
4. Each member of a scale is called a *degree* and is labeled by number.
5. Each scale degree also has a *scale degree name*.

A WORD OR TWO ABOUT MODE

Before we continue discussing scales, it's important to understand what a *mode* is. Think of the word mode as meaning *version*, a *variety* of some larger concept, or as a *manner* of doing something. For example, when we travel we pick a mode of transportation—a car, walking, the bus, an airplane—all are modes of traveling. On a specific level, each has different modes of operation: the plane may be cruising, landing, taxiing, etc.

Musically speaking, the general concept is to take the notes of the major scale and rotate them to create seven "versions" with the same pitches. As such, when we refer to the "modes of the major scale" we are pointing out all the possible ways the notes of the major scale can be ordered, and each specific "way" is called a mode of the major scale. Therefore, we can think of a mode as always having a "parent" scale.

On the specific level, the word "mode" is used to refer to the so-called "church" modes, which are used less often than the major and minor modes. Unfortunately the word "scale" is often mistakenly used interchangeably with mode, so there is potential for confusion.

THE MAJOR SCALE

Looking at the characteristics of a scale, let's construct one that meets all of the criteria. First we need seven pitches in alphabetical order:

TRACK 34

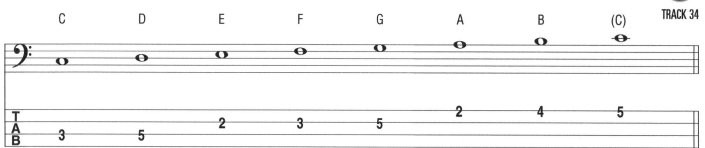

This collection contains seven consecutive step-wise pitches, and each has a different letter name. The C at the top indicates the next octave, which means this collection does not exceed one octave. Let's examine the order of half and whole steps in order to determine the mode:

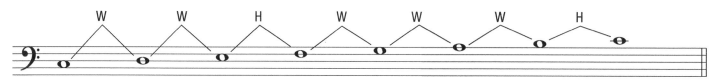

This is the pattern for a *major scale*, which can also be called the *major mode*.

The C major scale happens to have no sharps or flats next to any of the notes, and we say that all seven pitches are *diatonic* to the C major scale. Using a keyboard, you would only be playing the white keys.

Each member of the scale is a *degree* of the scale, and is labelled by a number with a caret above it.

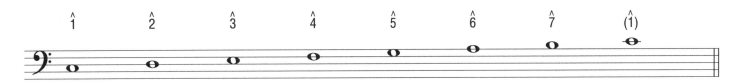

In addition to numbers, each scale degree has a *scale degree name* as well.

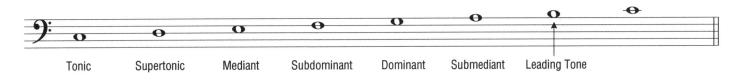

Looking at the scale degree names, some make perfect sense, while others may be confusing. For example, the dominant is $\hat{5}$, and the scale degree *beneath* it ($\hat{4}$) is called the *sub*dominant. But why is $\hat{6}$ called the *sub*mediant when it is above the mediant ($\hat{3}$)? Scale degree names are ordered by both going above and below the tonic by the same size interval. For example, a perfect 5th above the tonic, C, is the dominant, G. A perfect fifth below the tonic, C, is the pitch F—the subdominant. The following graphic illustrates this:

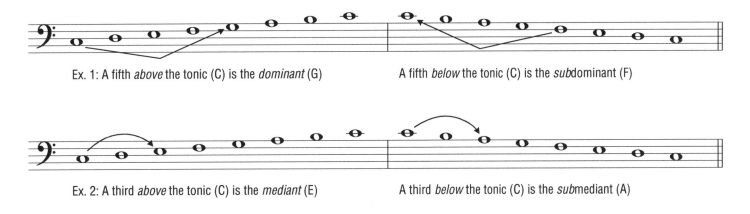

Ex. 1: A fifth *above* the tonic (C) is the *dominant* (G)   A fifth *below* the tonic (C) is the *sub*dominant (F)

Ex. 2: A third *above* the tonic (C) is the *mediant* (E)   A third *below* the tonic (C) is the *sub*mediant (A)

THE MINOR SCALE

The *minor scale* is almost identical to the major scale, except that the order of half and whole steps is slightly different.

TRACK 35

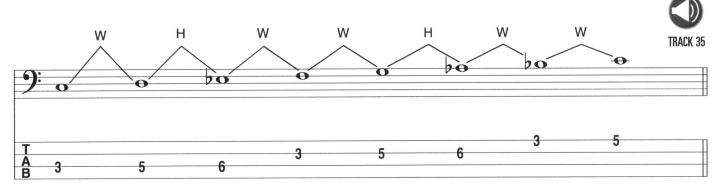

Comparing this to a major scale, we can see that $\hat{3}$, $\hat{6}$, and $\hat{7}$ of the minor scale are one half step lower than their major scale counterparts. Scale degree $\hat{7}$ is called the *subtonic* in the minor mode, owing to its whole-step distance from the tonic. Unlike the major scale however, there are a total of three varieties of minor scale. The one we've just seen is called the *natural minor* or *pure minor*. If we take a natural minor scale and raise $\hat{7}$ one half step (as it is in the major scale) it's called the *harmonic minor scale*. Its characteristic sound is the interval of an augmented 2nd (three half steps) between $\hat{6}$ and $\hat{7}$.

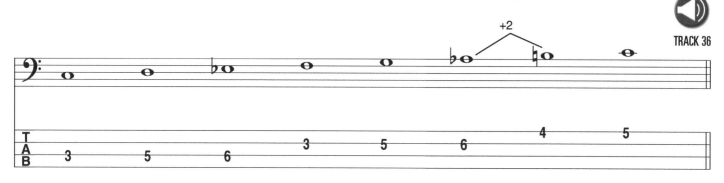

TRACK 36

If we take the harmonic minor scale and raise $\hat{6}$ one half step, it is called the *melodic minor scale*; the only difference between it and the major scale is a lowered $\hat{3}$.

TRACK 37

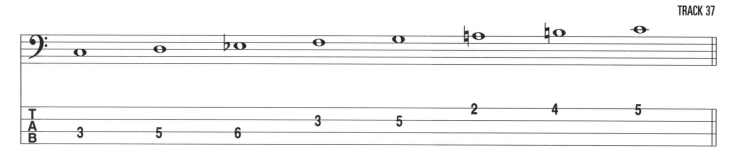

What these three minor scales all have in common is a lowered $\hat{3}$, and that is why we consider them all to be minor. But why have three different minor scales?

The three forms of the minor scale came out of compositional preferences and practices dating back hundreds of years. The harmonic minor, with the raised leading tone, provided a stronger connection to the tonic when the pitches were organized in chords. However, when the harmonic minor was played melodically rather than harmonically, the interval between $\hat{6}$ and $\hat{7}$ (an augmented 2nd) was unpleasing to the ear, so $\hat{6}$ was raised one half step as well when the melody approached the tonic by $\hat{6}$ and $\hat{7}$ consecutively in ascension. If a melody descended from the tonic, then most often the natural minor was used. Because of this, we say that the melodic minor scale has an ascending and a descending form.

TRACK 38

Ascending

Descending

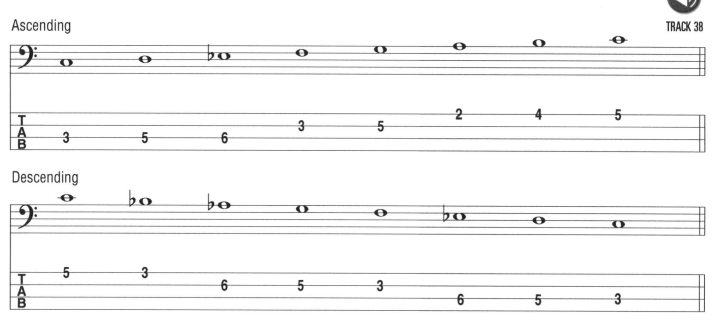

RELATIVE AND PARALLEL MINOR

For every major scale there is a minor scale that is made from the same set of pitches. For example, the C major scale (C–D–E–F–G–A–B–C) contains no sharps or flats, and the A minor scale (A–B–C–D–E–F–G–A) similarly has no accidentals. The A minor scale is said to be the *relative minor* of the C major scale. The word "relative" refers to the shared set of pitches (and as we will learn later, a shared *key signature*). There is only one relative minor per major scale and vice versa.

Let's look at the pattern of whole and half steps for major and minor scales. For this example I've written the pattern twice, indicating they are two octaves long. The top row is the pattern for major, and the bottom row is the pattern for minor:

```
        W   W   h   W   W   W   h | W   W   h   W   W   W   h
        W   h   W   W   h   W   W | W   h   W   W   h   W   W
```

Notice anything? Watch what happens when the bottom row (minor) is shifted two places to the left:

```
        W   W   h   W   W   W   h | W   W   h   W   W   W   h
    W   h   W   W   h   W   W | W   h   W   W   h   W   W
```

The pattern is exactly the same! This means that the relative minor can be found by starting on a certain scale degree of the major scale.

The tonic of the relative minor is a diatonic third below the tonic of the major scale. By using inversion, you could also choose a sixth above the tonic and arrive at the same scale degree, the submediant ($\hat{6}$). Using C major as the example, a diatonic third below the tonic is the pitch A, and a diatonic sixth above the tonic is also the pitch A.

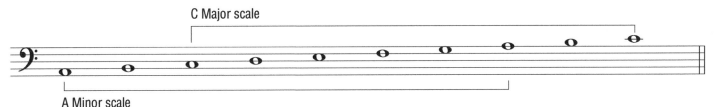

Applying the same formula to B♭ major, a diatonic third below B♭ is the pitch G, and a diatonic sixth above B♭ is also the pitch G. The relative minor of B♭ major is G minor.

This means if we order the pitches of the B♭ major scale (B♭–C–D–E♭–F–G–A–B♭) starting and ending on G ($\hat{6}$), we arrive at the G minor scale: G–A–B♭–C–D–E♭–F–G. Just as every major scale has a relative minor, every minor scale has a relative major. To find it, just reverse the process: go up a diatonic third or down a diatonic sixth from the tonic of a minor scale to find its relative major.

Bassist's Solution:

The relative minor (or relative major) is easy to find using the fingerboard. On the same string, the tonic of the relative minor is three frets lower than the tonic of the major scale, and vice versa. Using adjacent strings, the tonic of the relative minor is one string lower and two frets higher than the tonic of the major scale, and vice versa.

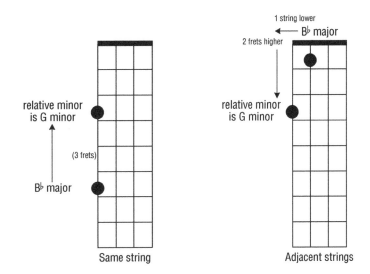

The *parallel minor* of a major scale is a minor scale that shares the same tonic pitch. For example the parallel minor of E major is E minor; the parallel minor of C major is C minor, etc. To summarize the difference between *relative* and *parallel minor*:

Relative Minor = same pitches, different tonic

Parallel Minor = same tonic, different pitches

THE MODES OF THE MAJOR SCALE

These "church" modes are part of a system devised during the Medieval era and expanded upon during the Renaissance. The first four modes to be recognized were called Dorian, Phrygian, Lydian, and Mixolydian. Later on the modes Aeolian and Ionian were added. A seventh modern mode, Locrian, completes the set. The modes appear in today's popular music, especially in jazz.

As the title of this section suggests, each of the seven modes can be derived from the major scale. You should first memorize the seven names in the following order, along with the respective number for each. You should be able to state the name of the mode when given its number, or state the number of the mode when given its name.

1. Ionian
2. Dorian
3. Phrygian
4. Lydian
5. Mixolydian
6. Aeolian
7. Locrian

Starting with the major scale as our point of reference we can create the modes by starting and ending on successive scale degrees. The first mode of the major scale, called Ionian, *is* the major scale.

$$\hat{1} \quad \hat{2} \quad \hat{3} \quad \hat{4} \quad \hat{5} \quad \hat{6} \quad \hat{7} \quad \hat{1}$$
$$C \quad D \quad E \quad F \quad G \quad A \quad B \quad C$$

Perhaps the best instrument with which to reinforce mode construction is the piano, so try working through this section on a keyboard as well as your bass. Now, instead of starting and ending the sequence with C ($\hat{1}$ to $\hat{1}$), let's run it from D to D ($\hat{2}$ to $\hat{2}$):

$$\hat{2} \quad \hat{3} \quad \hat{4} \quad \hat{5} \quad \hat{6} \quad \hat{7} \quad \hat{1} \quad \hat{2}$$
$$D \quad E \quad F \quad G \quad A \quad B \quad C \quad D$$

This is still a C major scale, only it's from D to D instead of C to C. In other words, this is a *manner* of expressing the C major scale, or better put, it is a *mode* of the C major scale. The name for this, the second mode of C major, is "D Dorian." The rest of the modes are based on each successive scale degree of the same "parent" scale—the major scale. This is why we call them the "modes of the major scale."

The following audio example demonstrates all seven modes of the C major scale. Look at the following chart as you listen:

TRACK 39

Mode Name	Built On	Degrees of Parent Scale	Letter Names
C Ionian (major)	Scale degree $\hat{1}$	$\hat{1}\ \hat{2}\ \hat{3}\ \hat{4}\ \hat{5}\ \hat{6}\ \hat{7}\ \hat{1}$	C D E F G A B C
D Dorian	Scale degree $\hat{2}$	$\hat{2}\ \hat{3}\ \hat{4}\ \hat{5}\ \hat{6}\ \hat{7}\ \hat{1}\ \hat{2}$	D E F G A B C D
E Phrygian	Scale degree $\hat{3}$	$\hat{3}\ \hat{4}\ \hat{5}\ \hat{6}\ \hat{7}\ \hat{1}\ \hat{2}\ \hat{3}$	E F G A B C D E
F Lydian	Scale degree $\hat{4}$	$\hat{4}\ \hat{5}\ \hat{6}\ \hat{7}\ \hat{1}\ \hat{2}\ \hat{3}\ \hat{4}$	F G A B C D E F
G Mixolydian	Scale degree $\hat{5}$	$\hat{5}\ \hat{6}\ \hat{7}\ \hat{1}\ \hat{2}\ \hat{3}\ \hat{4}\ \hat{5}$	G A B C D E F G
A Aeolian (minor)	Scale degree $\hat{6}$	$\hat{6}\ \hat{7}\ \hat{1}\ \hat{2}\ \hat{3}\ \hat{4}\ \hat{5}\ \hat{6}$	A B C D E F G A
B Locrian	Scale degree $\hat{7}$	$\hat{7}\ \hat{1}\ \hat{2}\ \hat{3}\ \hat{4}\ \hat{5}\ \hat{6}\ \hat{7}$	B C D E F G A B

You should, of course, practice building the seven modes of all the other major scales, not just C. In addition, it is crucial to be able to name the parent major scale for any possible mode. When given any mode name, for instance "F Mixolydian," you will:

1. State the number of the mode. (You should have them memorized.) In this case, Mixolydian is the 5th mode.

2. Assign the tonic of the mode (F) the *number* of the mode ($\hat{5}$).

3. Find the parent major scale by counting down the major scale formula, always keeping half steps from $\hat{3}$–$\hat{4}$ and $\hat{7}$–$\hat{8}$. In our example, if F is $\hat{5}$, the figure below shows that B♭ is $\hat{1}$, so the B♭ major scale is the parent of F Mixolydian.

4. Finally, play the parent major scale from the root of the mode. (Play B♭ major from F to F to get F Mixolydian.)

Major Scale Formula

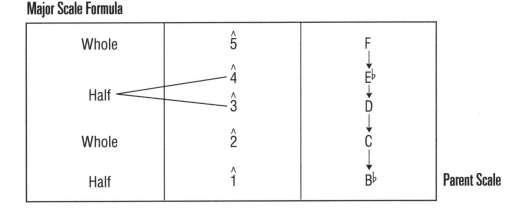

Review and practice this procedure with all the modes on various roots until the skill of finding the parent major scale becomes instantaneous. It's easy to get this mixed up at first, but persistence will be rewarded with a greater playing vocabulary.

AN ALTERNATIVE FORMULA FOR CONSTRUCTING MODES

In order to effectively apply them to bass line construction and soloing situations, we must also know the spelling, or particular order of half and whole steps, for each mode. With this in mind we can divide modes into two categories: modes that are *like* a major scale (with a major $\hat{3}$), and modes that are *like* a minor scale (with a minor $\hat{3}$). In most cases only one other scale degree is changed. Approaching modes this way means we need not be concerned at all about a parent major scale.

Modes like the major scale:

Lydian and Mixolydian

Modes like the minor scale:

Dorian, Phrygian, and Locrian

The Lydian mode is like a major scale except $\hat{4}$ is raised one half step. So we can say the formula for the Lydian mode is: $\hat{1}$–$\hat{2}$–$\hat{3}$–#$\hat{4}$–$\hat{5}$–$\hat{6}$–$\hat{7}$–$\hat{1}$.

C Lydian   TRACK 40

The Mixolydian mode is just like a major scale except $\hat{7}$ is lowered one half step. So we can say that the formula for the Mixolydian mode is: $\hat{1}$–$\hat{2}$–$\hat{3}$–$\hat{4}$–$\hat{5}$–$\hat{6}$–♭$\hat{7}$–$\hat{1}$.

C Mixolydian   TRACK 41

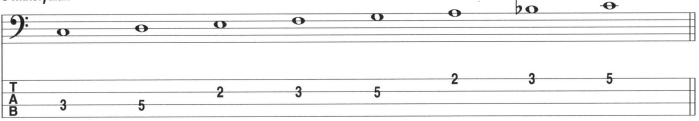

The Dorian mode is like a natural minor scale except $\hat{6}$ is raised one half step. So the formula for the Dorian mode is: $\hat{1}-\hat{2}-\flat\hat{3}-\hat{4}-\hat{5}-\hat{6}-\flat\hat{7}-\hat{1}$.

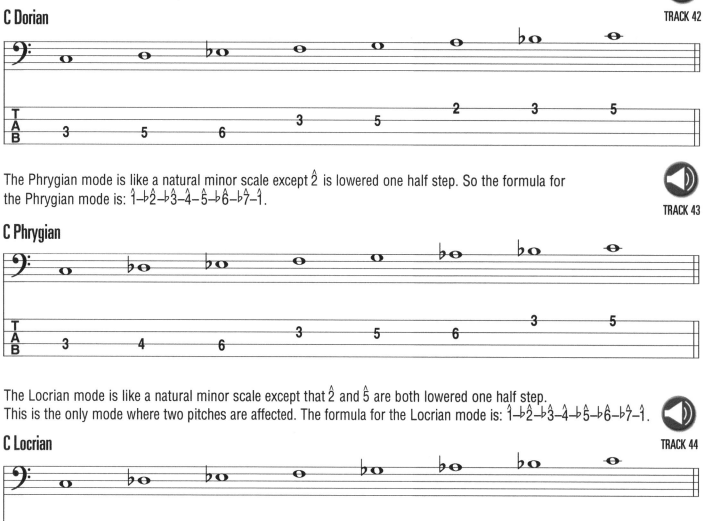

C Dorian

The Phrygian mode is like a natural minor scale except $\hat{2}$ is lowered one half step. So the formula for the Phrygian mode is: $\hat{1}-\flat\hat{2}-\flat\hat{3}-\hat{4}-\hat{5}-\flat\hat{6}-\flat\hat{7}-\hat{1}$.

C Phrygian

The Locrian mode is like a natural minor scale except that $\hat{2}$ and $\hat{5}$ are both lowered one half step. This is the only mode where two pitches are affected. The formula for the Locrian mode is: $\hat{1}-\flat\hat{2}-\flat\hat{3}-\hat{4}-\flat\hat{5}-\flat\hat{6}-\flat\hat{7}-\hat{1}$.

C Locrian

We've already seen the two remaining modes, Aeolian and Ionian. The Ionian mode is the major scale, or as we say, the major *mode*. The Aeolian mode is the natural minor scale, or the minor mode. This is where, as we said, sometimes the words "scale" and "mode" are used interchangeably.

QUESTIONS FOR REVIEW

1. What makes a *mode* different from or similar to a *scale*?

2. Are *relative minor* and *parallel minor* the same thing?

3. What do "like a major scale" and "like a minor scale" mean in reference to modes?

4. What is a "parent major scale?"

TOPICS FOR FURTHER STUDY

1. Exotic and ethnic scales and modes

2. Fingerings for all modes

CHAPTER 6: KEY

It was mentioned in Chapter 5 that the concept of *key* is closely related to the concepts of scale and mode. The notion of key further supports the meaning of tonality, as music "in a key" means that one pitch above all is the center of gravity, and the notes belonging to that key are considered *diatonic*. But if we have scales to tell us the same information, why bother with keys? Let's look at the D major scale:

As you can see, in order to maintain the proper pattern of whole steps and half steps for a major scale, a sharp is added to the notes F and C. Every time those notes appear, it's necessary for the performer to know they should be played as F♯ and C♯. Presuming the entire piece is written using only the notes from the D major scale, writing the accidentals in for every occurrence is unnecessary—the same information can be indicated with a *key signature*.

A key signature is an ordered collection of either sharps or flats (not a mixture) at the left of the staff. For our example, D major, there are two notes that require sharps next to them: F and C.

We can say that the key signature for D major has two sharps; every time the notes F and C appear on the staff (no matter what the octave), they are to be played as F♯ and C♯.

One of the great advantages of key signatures is that each major scale (and the key of the same name) has a specific number of sharps or flats that occur naturally. This means that each key can be identified simply by the number of accidentals in the key signature. In addition, each time we add a new accidental, we keep the ones that preceded it. For example, D major has two sharps, F♯ and C♯, and the key that has three sharps (which happens to be A major) has both F♯ and C♯ in its key signature, and adds a new sharp on the pitch G. And to drive the point home, the key that has four sharps (which happens to be E major) has in its key signature F♯, C♯, and G♯ (from the previous keys) and adds a fourth sharp on the pitch D, and so on.

There is an order of accidentals for both sharp and flat keys. For the sharp keys, the order is F–C–G–D–A–E–B. For the flat keys it's the reverse: B–E–A–D–G–C–F. Here are all of the major key signatures, written out first as scales, and then followed by the key signature. Remember that C major has no sharps or flats in the scale/key, so it's not included.

G Major

D Major

A Major

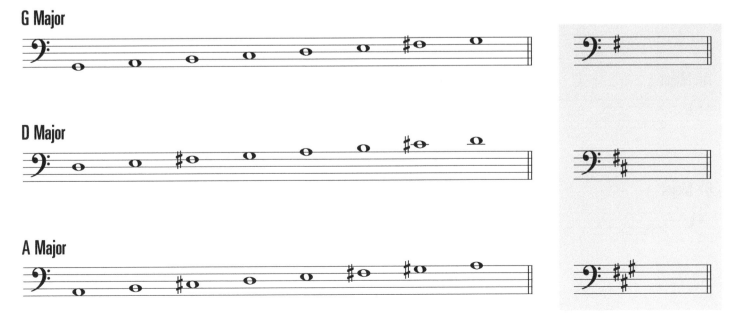

E Major

B Major

F# Major

C# Major

F Major

B♭ Major

E♭ Major

A♭ Major

D♭ Major

G♭ Major

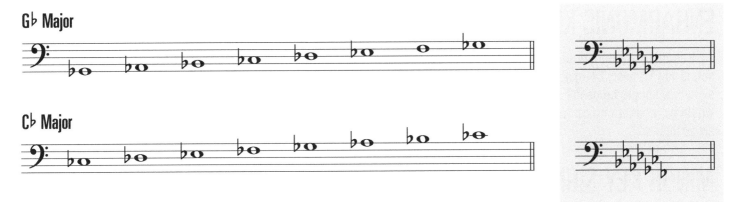

C♭ Major

IDENTIFYING KEYS

We've learned how to construct keys from scratch, but how do we identify the key by looking at the signature? There are handy tricks for both flat and sharp keys. For sharp keys, the very last sharp in the signature is the leading tone of the key ($\hat{7}$), meaning the pitch one half step above it is the tonic ($\hat{1}$). For example, the key signature for B major has five sharps, and the last sharp is the pitch A♯. One half step above A♯ is the pitch B, the tonic of the key.

For flat keys, the next-to-last flat in the signature is the name of the key. For example, the key signature for E♭ major is three flats. The next-to-last flat in the signature is E♭, which is the tonic of the key. One signature, F major with only one flat, won't work with this system so it will be up to you to memorize it. As you continually work with key signatures you will begin to memorize them all by number of accidentals and will no longer need these tricks.

THE CIRCLE OF FIFTHS

There is yet another way to appreciate the organization of key signatures, and thankfully this theory is consistent throughout. Starting with the key of C major, the order of major key signatures follows a pattern: the tonic of each successive key is a perfect 5th higher than the previous key. For example, start with C major (no sharps). A perfect 5th above C is the pitch G, and G major (1 sharp) is the next key signature. A perfect 5th above G is the pitch D, and D major (2 sharps) is the next key signature, etc.

What about the flats? The pattern for the flats is almost the same, but instead of going up a perfect fifth, you go down a perfect fifth. A perfect 5th down from C is the pitch F, and F major is the key signature with one flat. A perfect 5th below F is the pitch B♭, and B♭ major (2 flats) is the next key signature. If we organize all of the major key signatures this way, we end up with what's called the *circle of fifths*.

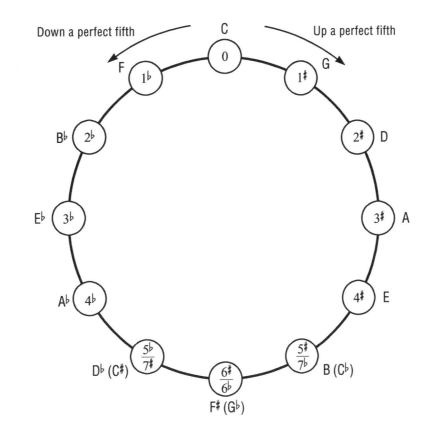

ENHARMONIC KEYS

Just as there are enharmonic pitches, there are enharmonic keys. At the bottom of the circle of fifths, G♭ major is equal in sound to F♯ major, C♭ major is equivalent in sound to B major, and C♯ major is equivalent in sound to D♭ major. Which key signature should be used? Applying the rule of thumb that simpler is always better, the key signature with fewer accidentals would be a better choice. In the case of G♭ major and F♯ major, the choice is up to personal preference since they both have six accidentals.

MINOR KEY SIGNATURES

We learned that every major scale has a relative minor scale. The same holds true for key signatures. Ultimately there are only twelve possible signatures, but they represent twenty-four keys: twelve major and twelve minor.

To review, we find the relative minor by starting from the tonic and either descending a diatonic third or ascending a diatonic sixth. In both cases we end up with $\hat{6}$, the submediant. Using D major as an example, a diatonic third below D is B. This means that the key signature for D major—two sharps—is also they key signature for *B minor.* This method is preferred since you don't have to memorize another twelve key signatures; learn the twelve major keys and then their relative minor keys. Below is the circle of fifths with major keys on the outside in uppercase and relative minor keys inside, in lowercase.

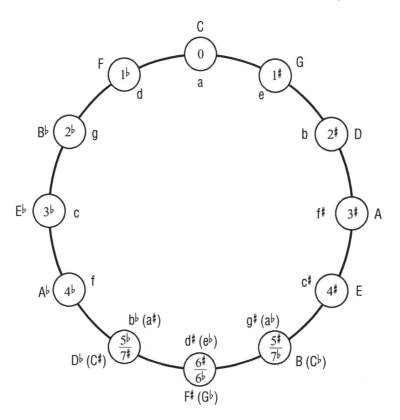

QUESTIONS FOR REVIEW

1. How are keys and scales related?

2. What does it mean to be "in a key?"

3. What is the *circle of fifths*, and why is it useful?

TOPICS FOR FURTHER STUDY

1. Modal key signatures

CHAPTER 7: SCALE AND MODE—PART II

This chapter is a collection of modern scales and modes that you are likely to encounter in rock, blues, and jazz. Although knowledge of these scales can be applied to the construction of bass lines, they are more often studied as resources for melodic improvisation.

All of the scales examined up to this point have consisted of seven different pitches. The scales in this chapter range from five to twelve pitches. It is important to memorize the traditional scales and modes described in Chapter 5, but it's not necessary to memorize the contents of this chapter in order to proceed to Chapter 8.

THE CHROMATIC SCALE

The *chromatic scale* contains all twelve pitches, arranged in half steps. Whether sharps or flats are used should be based on the direction of the scale. If the scale is ascending, use sharps; if it is descending, use flats.

C Chromatic

TRACK 45

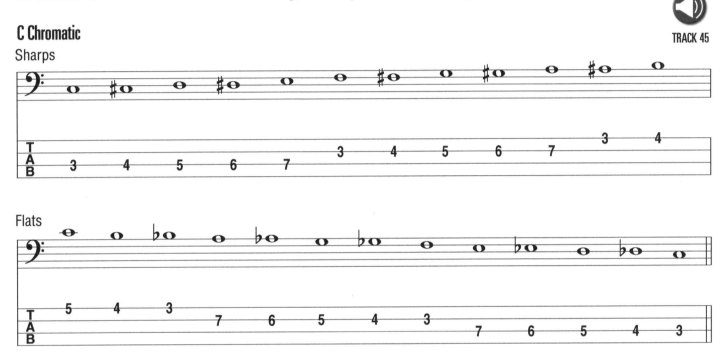

THE PENTATONIC SCALE

The *pentatonic scale* consists of five notes (from the Greek *pente*, meaning *five*) and is characterized by a lack of any half steps. There are a variety of pentatonic scale types, though the *major* and *minor pentatonic scales* are used most often. The major pentatonic scale is just like a major scale with $\hat{4}$ and $\hat{7}$ missing.

TRACK 46

C Major Pentatonic

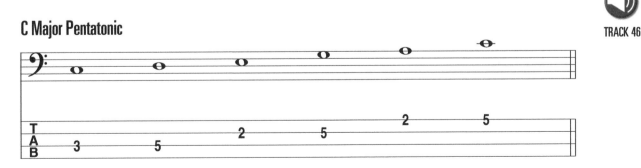

The minor pentatonic is similar to a minor scale, but scale degrees $\hat{2}$ and $\hat{6}$ are missing.

C Minor Pentatonic

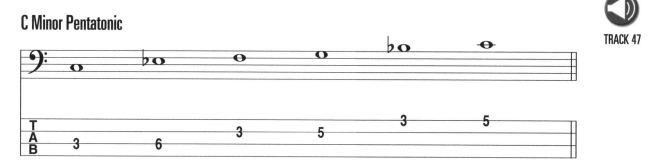

TRACK 47

THE BLUES SCALE

The *blues scale* is similar to a minor pentatonic scale with an added $\flat\hat{5}$.

C Blues

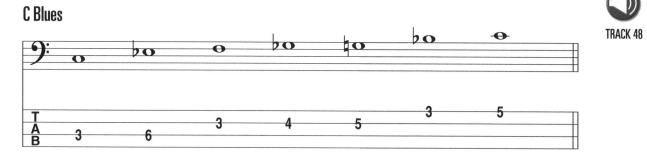

TRACK 48

Adding a $\natural\hat{7}$ to the blues scale creates the *altered blues scale*.

C Altered Blues

TRACK 49

SYMMETRICAL SCALES

As there are *symmetrical triads*—chords whose thirds are the same quality—so too are there *symmetrical scales*. There are two varieties of symmetrical scales: the *whole tone scale* and the *octatonic scale*.

The whole tone scale consists of six notes, each separated by a whole step. There are only two whole tone scales available; the rest are enharmonic spellings of one of the two.

C Whole Tone

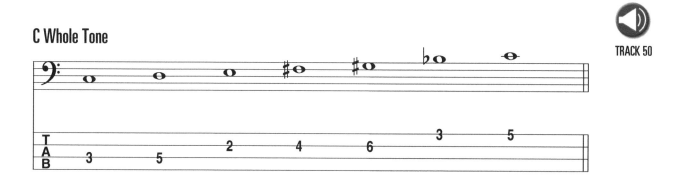

TRACK 50

The octatonic scale consists of eight notes separated by alternating half and whole steps. Since the scale can begin with either a whole step or a half step, there are two versions of the octatonic scale, which is also called the *diminished scale*. The first example begins by half step, and is referred to as the *half-whole diminished scale*:

C Half-Whole Diminished

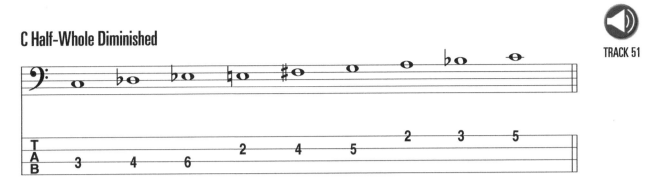

TRACK 51

The second example begins by whole step and is referred to as the *whole-half diminished scale*:

C Whole-Half Diminished

TRACK 52

You may have noticed that the rules concerning scales have to bend a little to accommodate the correct spelling of pitches in these scales. The octatonic scale may sometimes contain two scale degrees of the same letter name, for example, A♭ and A♮. The rules and formulas for scale construction almost always work out, and that is why we stick by them, but this is another example of music theory being a collection of guidelines for what happens in music *most* of the time.

MODES OF THE MELODIC MINOR AND HARMONIC MINOR SCALES

We can apply the same modal procedure—ordering a parent scale from successive scale degrees—to the harmonic minor scale and the melodic minor scale, creating their respective modes. The melodic and harmonic minor modes are used predominantly in jazz, particularly for melodic improvisation. How they apply to harmony, as well as theories and methods of improvisation, are beyond the scope of this book. The following is provided as a reference for learning the modes of harmonic and melodic minor, as well as the chords for which they are typically used.

Modes generated by the melodic minor and harmonic minor scales are named as altered versions of the major scale modes. For example, the second mode of the melodic minor scale is called Dorian ♭2, since it is identical to the Dorian mode except for a lowered $\hat{2}$. For this reason it's recommended that you memorize the modes of the major scale first, and learn these new modes as alterations of them. The only exception is mode seven of the melodic minor; it's called the altered dominant mode or scale, and sometimes the Superlocrian mode. You may find it easiest to learn to use this mode by thinking of it as "melodic minor up a half step" from the root of the altered dominant chord you want to play it over. We'll work on altered chords in Chapter 10.

Modes of the Melodic Minor Scale

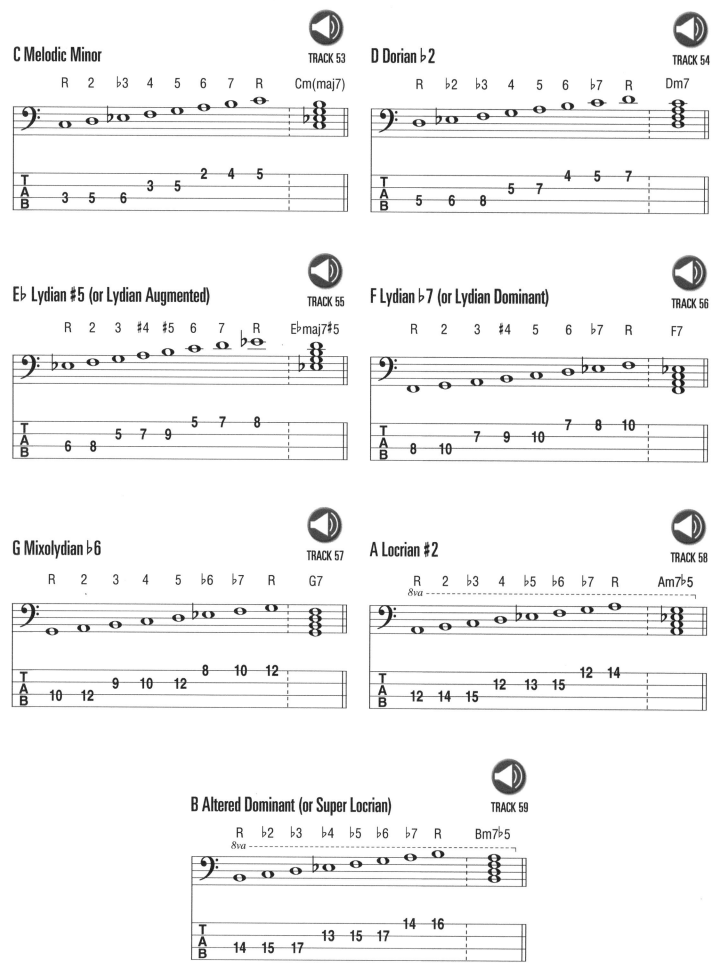

Modes of the Harmonic Minor Scale

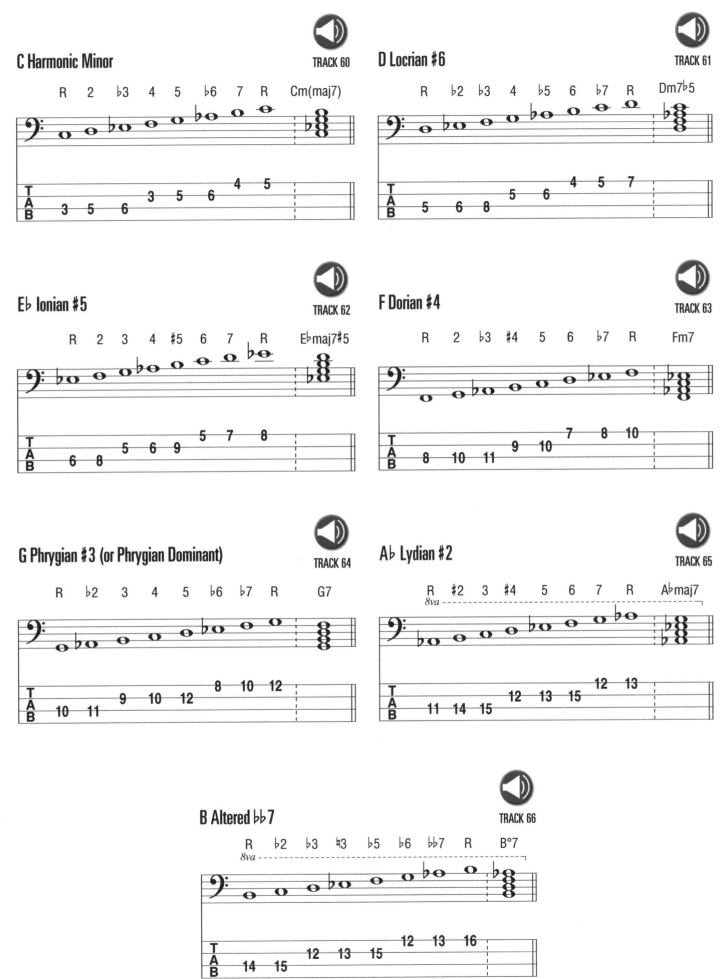

QUESTIONS FOR REVIEW

1. What makes a scale symmetrical?

2. How many different diminished scales are possible? How many whole tone scales?

3. Name types of scales that have other than seven pitches.

4. Which is the only church mode that has two altered scale degrees?

TOPICS FOR FURTHER STUDY

1. Modes of the major pentatonic scale

2. Fingerings for the chromatic scale

3. Olivier Messiaen and his "modes of limited transposition"

4. Emmett Chapman and his theory of the "Offset Modal System"

CHAPTER 8: RHYTHM AND METER

One of the characteristics that most distinguishes music from other forms of art is that it has a *temporal dimension*; music passes through time. In music, the most basic rhythmic unit is the *beat*, which can be even and steady or elusive and irregular. The combination of all characteristics involving time in music is referred to as *meter*.

The *pulse* of a composition refers to a continuous undercurrent of rhythmic iterations (beats) and can be perceived on various levels. For instance, we could be tapping our foot to the steady beat of a song and notice that the drummer is playing his hi-hat twice as fast as the beat. In that case, the hi-hat part is a *division* of the beat: it's cut in half and is played twice as fast. You could further *subdivide* the beat by tapping your hand four times as fast as the beat. The term "subdivide" is sometimes mistakenly used for all instances of rhythmic division. To subdivide something is to further divide it, meaning we first *divide* the beat then *sub*divide the beat. A subdivision then is necessarily at least two values removed from the beat.

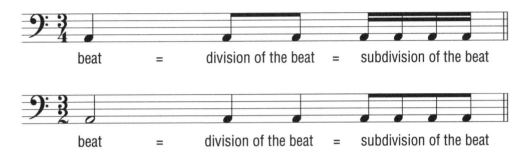

beat　　＝　　division of the beat　＝　subdivision of the beat

beat　　＝　　division of the beat　＝　subdivision of the beat

In nearly any composition, we always find something to tap our foot to, and it may not always be the pulse. For example, a rock drummer counts off four notes indicating the pulse, but as he or she plays we find ourselves only tapping our foot to beats one and three, or perhaps only two and four. The fancy term for this is the *tactus* (TOCK-toos), and it represents how we perceive the pulse. Keep in mind as we examine meter more thoroughly that our eyes may tell us what the beat is, but our ears tell us what the tactus is.

The relative fastness or slowness of the music refers to the *tempo*. Nowadays we usually use a metronome marking such as ♩ = 80 beats per minute, though for centuries a group of descriptive words such as *allegro, presto, adagio*, etc., were used to indicate the tempo.

TIME SIGNATURES

When we collect all of these elements together we express it as a *time signature*, also called a *meter signature*. The time signature indicates to us the beat, how it is grouped, and the number of them found per measure. A time signature is written as two numbers (one on top of the other) at the left of the staff, after the key signature.

There are two components to a time signature: how beats are *grouped*, and how they are *divided*. Beats are grouped at the tactus level and have descriptive names for each grouping: if there are two groups, we refer to the meter as *duple meter*, if there are three groups, *triple meter*, four groups is *quadruple meter*, etc.

The beat grouping can be divided in one of two ways: either evenly into two, which is called *simple meter*, or evenly into three, which is called *compound meter*.

For example, let's say that the quarter note is the beat and that there are two beats in a measure. A quarter note divides evenly into *two* eighth notes—this means that the meter is *simple*. Since there are two beats per measure, the meter is also *duple*. Therefore, the time signature of two quarter notes per measure is called *simple duple*.

Beat　　Divides into two
　　　　eighth notes (simple)

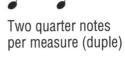

Two quarter notes
per measure (duple)

3) "Simple duple"

Instead of a quarter note for the beat, let's say that a *dotted* quarter note is the beat. A dotted quarter divides evenly into *three* eighth notes—this makes the meter *compound*. Therefore, with two beats per measure, and the beat is divisible by three, the meter is *compound duple*.

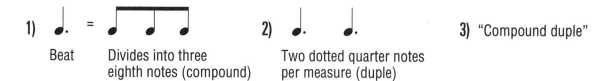

1) ♩. = ♪♪♪   2) ♩. ♩.   3) "Compound duple"

Beat   Divides into three   Two dotted quarter notes
        eighth notes (compound)   per measure (duple)

SIMPLE METERS

METER SIGNATURE	BEATS	DIVISIONS
$\frac{2}{2}$ = ¢		
$\frac{2}{4}$		
$\frac{2}{8}$		
$\frac{3}{2}$		
$\frac{3}{4}$		
$\frac{3}{8}$		
$\frac{4}{2}$		
$\frac{4}{4}$ = C		
$\frac{4}{8}$		

Simple Duple (rows 1–3)
Simple Triple (rows 4–6)
Simple Quadruple (rows 7–9)

Simple duple means that there are two beats in the measure and the beats are evenly divisible by two. *Simple triple* means there are three beats in the measure and the beats are evenly divisible by two. *Simple quadruple* means there are four beats in the measure and they are evenly divisible by two.

COMMON TIME AND CUT TIME

The time signature of 4/4 is often referred to as *common time*, for the simple reason that it is one of the most frequent (or *common*) time signatures found in music. On the staff it can be represented as a large "C" instead of using 4/4. The time signature of 2/2 is often called *cut time* due to the measure containing (and being felt in) only two beats, and is represented as a large "C" with a slash through the middle. Cut time is often used in Latin music.

Common Time

Cut Time

COMPOUND METERS

	METER SIGNATURE	BEATS	DIVISIONS
Compound Duple	6/4		
	6/8		
	6/16		
Compound Triple	9/4		
	9/8		
	9/16		
Compound Quadrulple	12/4		
	12/8		
	12/16		

Similarly to simple meters, *compound duple* means that there are two beats, though now the beats are evenly divisible by three. *Compound triple* means there are three beats and they are evenly divisible by three, and *compound quadruple* means there are four beats and they are evenly divisible by three, etc. Don't be too concerned about learning the names of these meters, instead, focus on what you're tapping your foot to and ask yourself this question: can it be divided by two or three? If it's two, the meter is simple, and if the answer is three, the meter is compound.

A TIME SIGNATURE CASE STUDY

Taking a look at the time signature of 6/8, and following the rule that the bottom number indicates which note equals one beat and the top number indicates the number of beats per measure, why would we call this a compound time signature? After all, eighth notes are divisible by two, not three! This is a perfect example of eyes vs. ears: When we hear 6/8, most often in a moderate to fast tempo, we tend to group the eighth notes into two groups of *three* (compound), rather than hearing six equal eighth note beats. Since there are two groups and they are divisible by three, it's called compound duple.

Just as with language, we cannot formalize every aspect of music's construction. We must be as consistent as possible while allowing music to be an art form, and this is exactly why it's called music *theory*.

ASYMMETRIC METERS

Last, there are time signatures that do not fall under these two categories, and we call them *asymmetric meters.* For example, we may find five or seven beats per measure, and they are usually grouped asymmetrically. In the case of five beats per measure, we usually group them 2 + 3 or 3 + 2, in the case of seven, 4 + 3 or 3 + 4, or further to 2 + 2 + 3. All of these numbers are then written over the beat value.

TIES

A tie—a curved line drawn from notehead to notehead—means that the second of the tied notes is not articulated. Instead, the attack of the first note is sustained through its value. More than one note can be tied, including notes in multiple measures, and the value is held through all of the tied notes. When a note is to be increased by less than half its duration, a tie must be used instead of a dot (a). Dots may take the place of ties both between and within beats, making the notation much simpler. Ties, on the other hand, are never drawn within the beat, such as between three eighth notes starting on beat 1 in a simple meter. Instead you would write this rhythm as their combined value, a dotted quarter note.

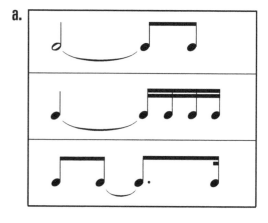

a.

As a general rule, the choice between dots and ties should be dictated by which makes the overall pulse clear. In 4/4 time, for instance, make sure beat 3 is visible in all cases, which may require the use of a tie.

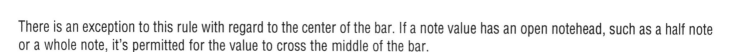

There is an exception to this rule with regard to the center of the bar. If a note value has an open notehead, such as a half note or a whole note, it's permitted for the value to cross the middle of the bar.

BEAMS

Notes are beamed within the beat because it simplifies the notation and helps illustrate the grouping of the time signature. The time signatures 6/8 and 3/4 both have six eighth notes per measure, but as we've learned, the former is a compound signature, while the latter is a simple signature. Beaming helps distinguish the two.

You can connect notes across several beats as long as the first note in that beam falls on a beat.

If you have a measure where the time is divided evenly by two, a beam should never cross in the center of the bar.

incorrect   correct

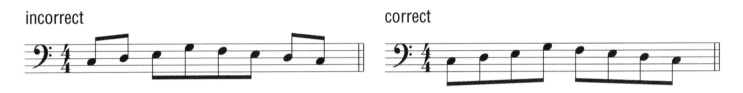

Ultimately, all beaming should be used to show the beats and visually reinforce the time signature. Mistakes happen most often in compound signatures.

incorrect   correct

TUPLETS AND BORROWED DIVISION

A *tuplet* is used when a beat is evenly divided contrary to its signature. For example, in 4/4, the beat is equally divided by two. If we want to equally divide the beat by three, we group the three notes with a beam and place a number "3" above or below it. This is called a *triplet*. You may encounter a triplet written as a ratio, for example 3:2, meaning 3 eighth notes in the space and time of 2 eighth notes.

The reverse is true in compound meters. In 6/8, where the beat is divided by three, if we want only two notes in the space and time of three notes, we group them with a beam and write a 2 above or below. This is called a *duplet*.

The beaming of tuplets follows the same rules for beaming regular notes: show the beats. Triplets and duplets are examples of *borrowed division*, meaning we are borrowing from one grouping (simple) and placing it in the grouping of another meter (compound), or vice versa. If a piece is made up predominantly of either triplets or duplets, it would make more sense to change the time signature.

Tuplets can occur in any size: quadruplets, quintuplets, septuplets, etc., the underlying theory being that the notes grouped within the tuplet must fit within the indicated beat's time, in accordance with the time signature. The following example shows fourteen sixteenth notes are to be played in a space where only twelve would occur naturally in the time signature:

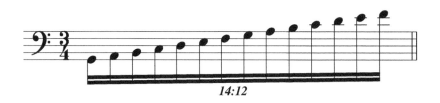

SYNCOPATION AND HEMIOLA

Each beat of a measure can be described as strong or weak. The chart below illustrates the relationship of strong to weak beats depending on the time signature:

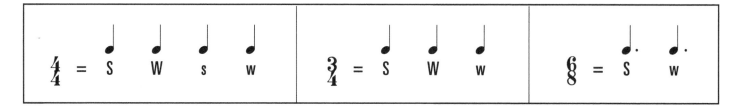

Strong beats receive an added stress and help us further to group beats and measures. Normally, notes that fall on the beat are considered strong, and those off the beat are considered weak. If a weak part of the beat suddenly gets stressed, we call the beat *syncopated*.

From time to time a figure in duple meter may be written in a triple meter pulse, and vice versa. This is called a *hemiola*, and it can occur both within and across bars.

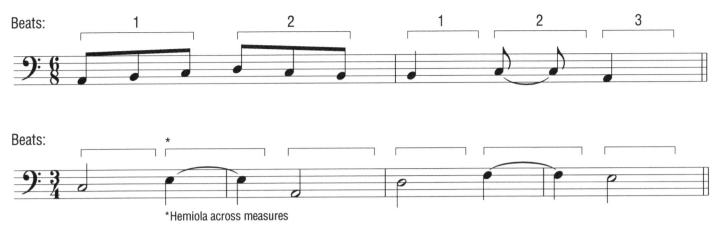

*Hemiola across measures

POLYRHYTHM AND POLYMETER

A *polyrhythm*, also called a *cross rhythm*, occurs when a figure goes against the predominant meter, and the two don't share the same pulse. In this example, the meter is three quarter notes per measure, and the figure requires four notes in the same measure:

Polymeter simply means multiple meters. For example, in a group setting the guitar may be written in 4/4 and the bass written in 3/4, meaning that phrases are based on groups of four beats in the guitar part and on groups of three in the bass part. A result is that the bar lines will not always fall in the same place, but they share the same beat and will eventually resolve: four measures of 3/4 (twelve beats total) is equal to three measures of 4/4 (twelve beats total). A subtle and simpler example would be a guitarist and bassist both playing in 6/8, with the guitarist grouping the beat in 2 + 4 and the bassist grouping the beat in 4 + 2.

QUESTIONS FOR REVIEW

1. What is the difference between the *tactus* and the *beat*?

2. What is the *subdivision* of an eighth note?

3. What is the main difference between *simple* and *compound meter*?

TOPICS FOR FURTHER STUDY

1. Polyrhythm and polymeter

2. Inégal rhythm

3. Metric modulation

CHAPTER 9: CHORDS—PART I

Knowledge of harmony is essential for the bassist; it is the tapestry that serves as the backdrop for bass lines. We can consider the bass line as a linear unfolding (horizontal) of the harmony (vertical), no matter what the style or genre. Building on the concept of intervals brings us logically to chords. A *chord*, by definition, is the simultaneous playing of three or more notes— though just as with intervals, we can play them melodically, creating what's called a *broken chord* or *arpeggio*.

Bassists seldom play chords, chiefly because of the size and breadth of the bass neck, but also because harmonic intervals in too low a register can sound very muddy. Not to mention, chord playing isn't the primary job of the bassist. However, some creative effects can be achieved by playing chords on the bass. Below is an example of a chord progression played on bass harmonically, then played again with some melodic tones in between the chords, giving the illusion of a walking bass line while *comping* (short for *accompanying*) the chords:

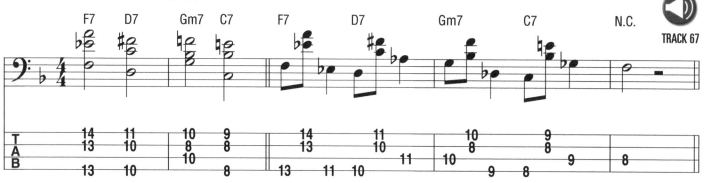

If a chord consists of three pitches only, it is called a *triad* (*tri* being the prefix for *three*). A triad is built with consecutive intervals of a third, and their differing combinations indicate the triad's quality (just like intervals). Chords consisting of thirds are described as being *tertian* chords—the basis of Western harmony.

There are two traditional ways to construct a triad: as a pair of thirds, or as a fifth surrounding a third; either method will give you the same result.

TRIADS AS A PAIR OF THIRDS

First, place a note a third above the starting pitch (called the *root*), and another note a third above the second pitch. You'll notice that the notes will all be on lines, or all on spaces. Triads come in four different qualities: augmented, major, minor, and diminished. If we think of a triad as two successive thirds, then we can define the qualities this way:

1. An augmented triad has two major 3rds.
2. A major triad has a major 3rd on the bottom, and a minor 3rd on top.
3. A minor triad has a minor 3rd on the bottom, and a major 3rd on top.
4. A diminished triad has two minor 3rds.

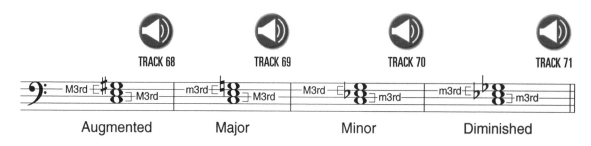

Augmented and diminished triads are called *symmetrical triads* because the size and quality of their intervals are all equal.

50

TRIADS AS A FIFTH SURROUNDING A THIRD

The interval from the bottom note to the top note of a triad is a fifth, so we can also describe triads as having a third above the bass and a fifth above the bass. Using this method, triads are defined this way:

1. An augmented triad has a major 3rd and an augmented 5th above the bass.

2. A major triad has a major 3rd and a perfect 5th above the bass.

3. A minor triad has a minor 3rd and a perfect 5th above the bass.

4. A diminished triad has a minor 3rd and a diminished 5th above the bass.

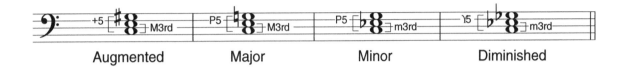

| Augmented | Major | Minor | Diminished |

This might be easier to remember since each chord quality shares its name with one of the intervals it contains (e.g. a diminished triad is the only one with a diminished 5th). Above all, learn to associate the *sound* of a triad with its quality.

You may have noticed a pattern that emerges with regard to scales and chords: to construct any chord, choose every other note of the scale—this guarantees that the triads will be made entirely of thirds. For example, in the key of C major, and starting with the pitch C, skip $\hat{2}$ and choose E ($\hat{3}$), skip $\hat{4}$ and choose G ($\hat{5}$). This creates the tonic triad C–E–G. Creating triads in this manner will always result in diatonic triads (i.e. they belong to the key).

A Roman numeral is used to indicate the scale degree upon which a chord is built. Capital Roman numerals are used for major and augmented triads, and lowercase Roman numerals are used for minor and diminished triads. The following example illustrates the diatonic triads of C major, though this pattern will generate diatonic triads in any major key:

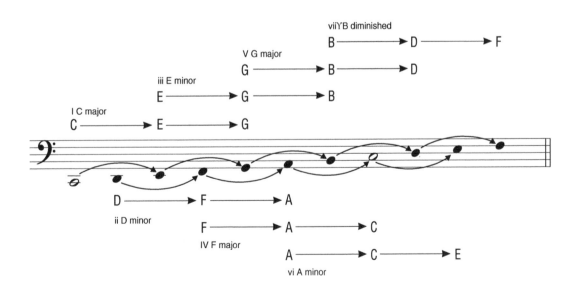

In a major key, the I, IV, and V triads are always major, and the ii, iii, and vi triads are always minor. The only diminished triad is vii°. There are no diatonic augmented triads in a major key.

There is a similar pattern for triads diatonic to the minor scale: the minor triads are i, iv, and v, the major triads are III, VI, and VII, and the remaining chord is diminished: ii°.

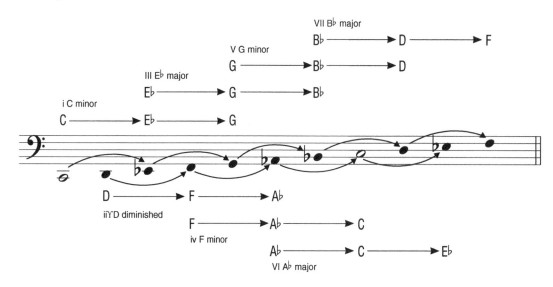

Taking the theory of relative major and minor into account, the order of chord qualities remains consistent; only the Roman numeral placement changes. Below is the diatonic order of triads in a major key, and below it the same for a minor key. The rows are offset by a third: the distance between relative major and minor.

	M	m	m	M	M	m	d	M	M	m	m	M
Major key	I	ii	iii	IV	V	vi	vii°	I	ii	iii	IV	V
Minor key	III	iv	v	VI	VII	i	ii°	III	iv	v	VI	VII
	C	Dm	Em	F	G	Am	B°	C	Dm	Em	F	G

C major scale

A minor scale

CHORD POSITION: INVERSION

The position of a chord is determined by the lowest chord tone (called the bass). How the tones of a chord are positioned and spaced is referred to as its *voicing*. It is important to understand that the bass and the root are not necessarily the same thing. The root can be the bass (when the tonic of the chord is the lowest note), but the bass isn't always the root. When it isn't, the chord is said to be *inverted*.

A triad is said to be in *root position* when the tonic of the chord is in the bass. A triad is said to be in *first inversion* when the third of the chord is in the bass. Last, a triad is said to be in *second inversion* when the fifth of the chord is in the bass. It does not matter how much space occurs between the bass and the rest of the chord tones; it is the bass and the bass alone that determines the position of the triad.

Placement of the pitches above the bass no more than one chord tone apart is called *close* voicing. Conversely, if there is more than one chord tone's space between notes, it is called an *open* voicing. The following are various positions and voicings of a C major triad:

close   open   close   open

Ultimately, open and close voicing is a distinction that won't matter a great deal to a bassist, though in the instance when you may voice chords yourself you'll notice more often than not that open voicing is required in order to prevent a muddled sound.

In close voicing, we can see what intervals are generated above the bass in each position. In root position, there is a third and a fifth above the bass, represented as $\frac{5}{3}$.

TRACK 72

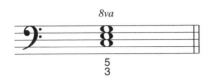

To make an inversion, take the bass note, and place it an octave higher. When the triad is in first inversion, there is a sixth and a third above the bass, represented as $\frac{6}{3}$.

TRACK 73

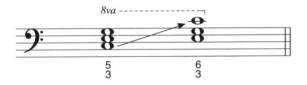

Last, second inversion has a sixth and a fourth above the bass, represented as $\frac{6}{4}$.

TRACK 74

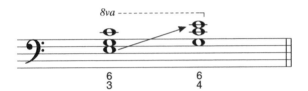

These symbols are called *figured bass*, which was originally found in *basso continuo* parts, a system used primarily in the Baroque era as a means of indicating the intervals above the written bass line to the keyboard player or whoever was playing the chords (the *continuo* instruments). It is a kind of musical shorthand used rather than writing out every single note in the music. Though the practices of the day were rather rigid, figured bass also permitted considerable variety, as the voicings of the chords were up for grabs. Today we use *slash notation* rather than figured bass. For example, a C triad in first inversion is written **C/E**, and the same chord in second inversion is written **C/G**. Root position is written solely as **C**: it is assumed that the chord is in root position when no slash appears.

CHORD POSITION: TEXTURE

Though all the notes of a chord are present regardless of its position, each nonetheless possesses unique textural characteristics. The differences can be placed in one of two categories: how stable the chord sounds (its tendency to stay put), or how unstable the chord sounds (its tendency to move to another chord position or a new chord all together).

Root position is the most stable sounding, owing in part to the perfect 5th found in the chord (between the tonic and the fifth of the chord). Below is a I–IV–V–I chord progression with each chord performed in root position. The progression is played twice on the track; the second time has the bass removed so you can play along.

TRACK 75

C	F	G	C
I	IV	V	I

C	F	G	C
I	IV	V	I

First inversion is less stable than root position and is often used as a connecting position to the subdominant. This position has a rather colorful sound to it, and if used too often, tends to sound less stable. In the next example, the same progression is used, but the tonic chord appears each time in first inversion: I $\frac{6}{3}$–IV–V–I $\frac{6}{3}$. At the end of the example, does it sound like the bass should stay in this position? When you play it yourself, try playing the final chord in first inversion and then in root position, and decide which sounds more stable.

TRACK 76

Second inversion is even less stable and should be used sparingly. It is used most often as either a pedal tone or when the dominant chord comes after the tonic chord. The example starts with the I chord in root position, then the IV chord in second inversion, then the V chord in first inversion: I–IV $\frac{6}{4}$–V $\frac{6}{3}$–I. The second time through the progression, the track features predominantly root position triads except at the end, where the V chord is prepared by the tonic chord, and then ends on the tonic: I–IV–I $\frac{6}{4}$–V–I.

TRACK 77

SEVENTH CHORDS

Chords consisting of four notes, built in thirds, are called *seventh chords*, because the fourth chord tone is an interval of a seventh above the root (when the chord is in root position). Just as with triads, seventh chords come in a variety of qualities as well as names. The names of seventh chords are very descriptive but can also be long and cumbersome, therefore there is a collection of practical symbols to represent them.

As with triads, we could think of seventh chords as a series of thirds stacked on one another, but memorizing all of those combinations is entirely too much work and impractical. Instead, think of a seventh chord in two parts: a triad and an added seventh interval above the bass. There are a variety of seventh chords in use in Western tonal music, and some are used more than others. The chart below lists the possibilities: the two-word name describes the quality of the triad (first word) and the added seventh interval (second word). The second column is a shorthand abbreviation of the two-word name, the third column is the practical name as it is used today, and the fourth column contains the symbol(s) associated with the chord used in lead sheets.

Triad + Interval	Abbreviation	Usually Called	Symbol
major-minor 7	maj(m7)	Dominant 7	C7
major-major 7	maj(maj7)	Major 7	Cmaj7, C△7
minor-minor 7	m(m7)	Minor 7	Cm7
diminished-minor 7	dim(m7)	Half-diminished 7	Cm7♭5, Cø7
diminished–diminished 7	dim(dim7)	Fully-diminished 7	C°7
augmented-major	aug(maj7)	Major 7 sharp 5	Cmaj7♯5
minor-major	m(maj7)	Minor/major 7	Cm(maj7)

Below is each type of seventh chord mentioned, all built with the note C as the root. Row A corresponds to the second column, Row B to the third column, and Row C to the fourth column from the previous table.

A:	maj(m7)	maj(maj7)	m(m7)	dim(m7)	dim(dim7)	aug(maj7)	m(maj7)
B:	Dominant 7	maj 7	minor 7	half–diminished 7	diminished 7	Maj7♯5	minor/Major 7
C:	7	maj 7	m7	m7♭5, ø7	°7	maj7♯5	m(maj7)

As with triads, each degree of the major and minor scale can be harmonized as a seventh chord.

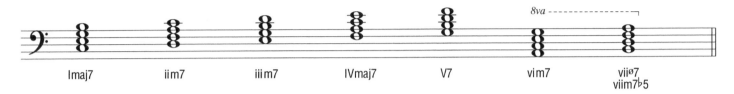

Imaj7   iim7   iiim7   IVmaj7   V7   vim7   viiø7
                                                  viim7♭5

SEVENTH CHORDS: INVERSION

The inversion of seventh chords works much in the same way as with triads, though there is an additional position due to the added pitch. The figured bass symbols for seventh chords contain three numbers to reflect the pitches above the bass, though we don't use all of them, just as we abbreviated the inversion of triads. Root position has a seventh, a fifth, and a third above the bass, though it is most often represented with the numeral 7 after the root name.

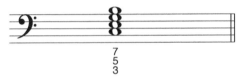

First inversion has a sixth, a fifth, and a third above the bass, usually represented as $\frac{6}{5}$.

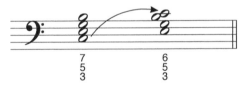

Second inversion has a sixth, a fourth, and a third above the bass, usually represented as $\frac{4}{3}$.

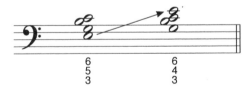

Third inversion has a sixth, a fourth, and a second above the bass, usually represented as $\frac{4}{2}$, or simply as a 2 after the chord name.

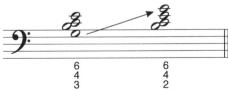

Slash notation for seventh chords follows the same convention established with triads, though you must be sure to include the quality of the chord before the slash. For example, a root-position Cmaj7 chord should be written as Cmaj7, first inversion as Cmaj7/E, second inversion as Cmaj7/G, and third inversion as Cmaj7/B.

At this point it's important to note that the pitch on the right side of the slash doesn't always have to be a chord tone, it can simply be an indication by the composer of the bass note that is desired under the chord. You could come across something like Cmaj7 with A♭ in the bass, written as Cmaj7/A♭. Since A♭ is not part of a Cmaj7 chord, we would not consider Cmaj7/A♭ to be an inversion. It's a simplified spelling of a more complex chord—in this case, A♭maj7♯9♯5.

QUESTIONS FOR REVIEW

1. Are chords often played on bass? Why or why not?

2. How many notes are in a *triad*?

3. What is the difference between a capital roman numeral and a lowercase roman numeral?

4. What does *voicing* mean?

TOPICS FOR FURTHER STUDY

1. Quartal and secundal harmony

2. Planing

3. Linear harmony

4. Bichords

CHAPTER 10: CHORDS—PART II

The chords we've examined so far are the fundamental types found in almost every style of music. The chords in this chapter extend the formula of stacking in thirds, resulting in what are called *extended chords* or *tall chords*. Jazz is where we are most likely to see chords such as ninths, elevenths, and thirteenths, as well as the sixth, add9, and suspended chords. Pop music as well as funk/R&B often feature these rich and colorful chords.

The number of chord tones in extended chords can be as many as seven—far too many for a bassist, and even for a guitarist! There are chord tones that can be omitted though, and it won't affect the overall quality of the chord's sound. The first pitch that can be omitted is the fifth; though it adds stability, in most chords it does not determine its quality. The following example is root–5–♭7, then the same chord voiced root–♭3–♭7. Without the third, the chord loses its quality, but it doesn't lack much when the fifth is omitted.

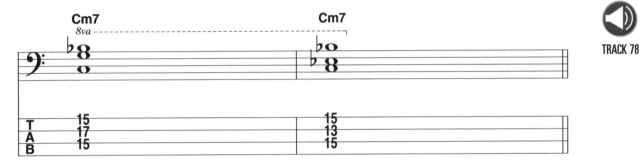

TRACK 78

Remember that the ninth, eleventh, and thirteenth are *compound* intervals: they are the octave equivalent of the second, fourth, and sixth. To find the pitches associated with a chord's extension, simply subtract seven from the number to get the scale degree within the first octave. Each chord is featured on the track in the form of a short groove beneath the chords played on piano and is repeated without the bass part so you can play along.

SIXTH CHORDS

The major and minor 6th chords both feature an added major 6th above the root. A sixth chord functions much in the same way as a triad with the same root; the sixth just adds some color. Looking at C6 (C–E–G–A), notice that it is comprised of the same notes as Am7 in first inversion… so which is it? The bassist decides by choosing which note is played in the bass. By voicing the chord with a low C, the ear is convinced C is the root rather than A. If A is the lowest note, then Am7 is the perceived chord.

TRACK 79

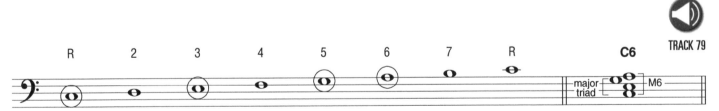

The minor 6th chord in root position, similarly, is the same as a half-diminished chord in first inversion. Again, the lowest bass note as well as the context persuade the ear as to which chord is being expressed.

TRACK 80

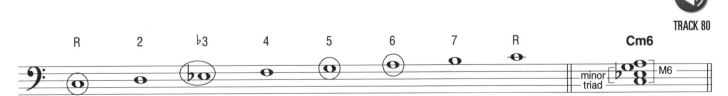

This is an excellent example of chord name versus chord function. As was mentioned earlier, a chord's name indicates what it *is* (the pitch it's based on, the quality, etc.), while the chord's function indicates what it *does*. If this chord was meant to function as a half-diminished chord, then we would have certain expectations as to the chord to follow: most likely it would be a dominant chord. If the chord was meant to function as a tonic minor 6th chord, then there are a few more choices available, such as the mediant, submediant, and dominant. Ultimately, context determines a chord's function.

NINTH CHORDS: MAJOR, MINOR, AND DOMINANT

The major 9th chord is a major 7th chord with a major 9th added above the root.

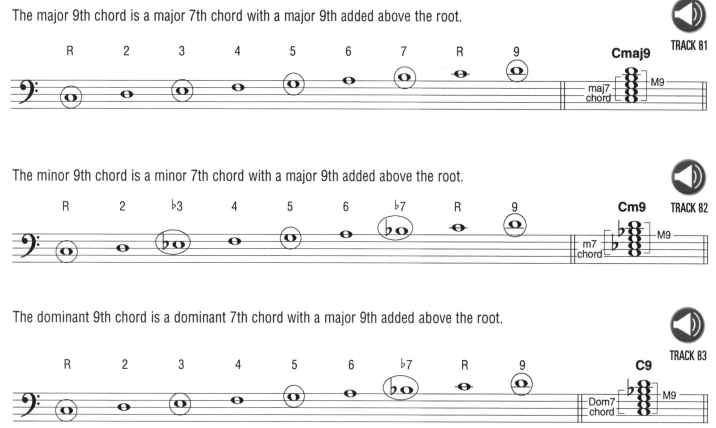

ELEVENTH CHORDS: MINOR AND DOMINANT

A dissonance occurs in a major 11th chord between the third and the eleventh (they are a half step apart when voiced in the same octave), so major 11th chords are generally avoided. A minor 11th chord is like a minor 9th chord with a perfect 11th added on top.

A dominant 11th chord is a dominant 9th chord with a perfect 11th added above the root.

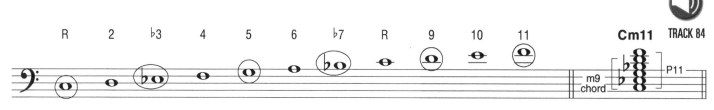

THIRTEENTH CHORDS: MAJOR, MINOR, AND DOMINANT

In a major 13th chord the eleventh is omitted for the same reason we don't see a major 11th chord: the dissonance between the third and the eleventh. The major 13th is a major 9th chord with an added major 13th above the root.

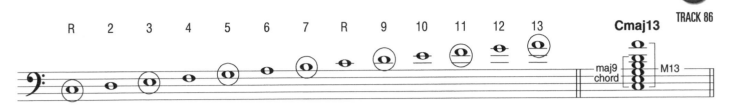

The minor 13th chord also omits the eleventh, though it is usually for reasons of playability by the guitarist. It is a minor 9th chord with an added major 13th above the root.

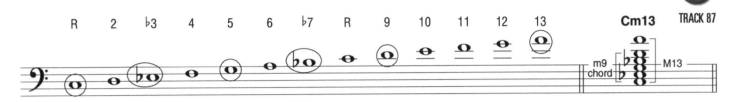

The dominant 13th also omits the eleventh for the same reason as the major 13th. The dominant 13th chord is a dominant 9th chord with an added major 13th above the root.

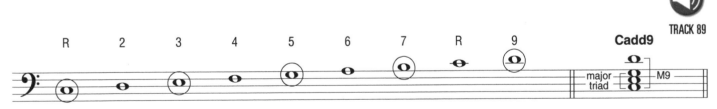

ADD9 CHORDS: MAJOR AND MINOR

An add9 chord is a triad with a major 9th added above the root and is comprised of only four notes. This is not to be confused with a ninth chord, which has a seventh included in the chord. The major add9 chord is a major triad with a major 9th added above the root.

The minor add9 chord is a minor triad with a major 9th added above the root.

SUSPENDED (SUS) CHORDS

The word *suspension* comes from classical music terminology. In that context a suspension is a tone whose natural progression is rhythmically delayed, creating dissonance with the chord that follows. The suspended note could be any note that creates such a dissonance, though most commonly it is the fourth or second, which at some point would resolve to the third.

In modern popular music, any chord without a third but including a second or fourth is called a *sus* chord. Further, suspended chords are considered neither major nor minor and don't have to resolve to their parent chords, maintaining tension until the next chord whether the suspension is resolved or not. Suspended chords can be found everywhere from jazz to pop to rock. A sus2 chord contains the root, second, and fifth.

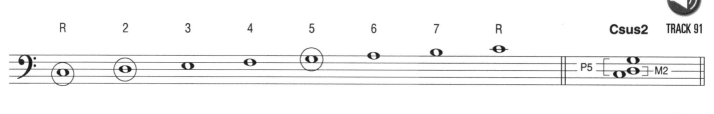

A sus4 chord contains the root, fourth, and fifth.

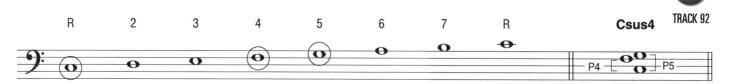

ALTERED DOMINANT CHORDS

An altered dominant chord is a dominant seventh chord with one or more of the following altered tones: ♭5, ♯5, ♭9, ♯9. A dominant 7♭5 is a dominant seventh chord with the fifth lowered one half step.

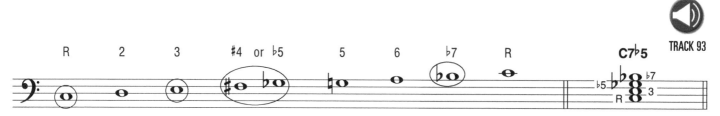

A dominant 7♯5 is a dominant seventh chord with the fifth raised one half step.

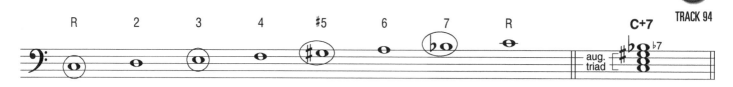

A dominant 7♭9 is a dominant 7th chord with an added lowered ninth. It's especially useful to recognize that the third, fifth, ♭7th, and ♭9th form a diminished 7th chord.

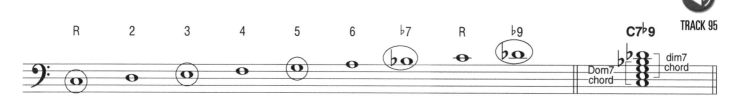

A dominant 7♯9 is a dominant 7th chord with an added raised 9th. This chord is sometimes referred to as a "split third" chord because it simultaneously contains both major and minor sonorities. The major third is an E♮, the minor third is an E♭—but spelled enharmonically as D♯.

TRACK 96

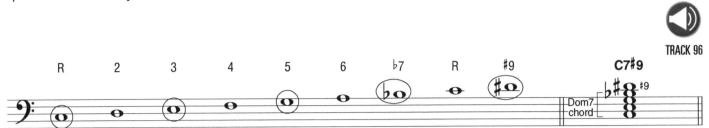

CODA

THE PURPOSE AND VALUE OF MUSIC THEORY

Have you ever heard someone say something like, "just because it's theoretically correct doesn't mean it's good," or, "you don't need theory to write good music." These statements aren't necessarily false, though they are true for reasons other than what was intended. One of my goals for this book was to explain that music theory is a *system for organizing*, not a tool used for evaluating. It's not called music *law* or music *fact*, it's called music *theory*: a complex suggestion that explains what happens in music more often than not. There is no relationship between music theory and the appraisal of music—those defensive statements like the ones I mentioned earlier often come from those who haven't yet learned theory and feel they've been asked to justify their music as to why it may "break the rules." There's no such thing as "right" or "wrong" music. Music theory no more evaluates music than English grammar appraises poetry. In fact, it's when rules are creatively and knowingly broken that we often feel a poem or piece of music has a beautiful, transcendent quality to it. But "rules" aren't usually broken for the sake of it; rather they're a point of reference—a launching pad for new ideas.

Don't get caught up in the trap of trying to prove that something you don't like is right or wrong—it's not possible, and more importantly, there's no value in determining such things. The power music holds over us is tied into our emotional response to it, and at the end of the day, theory or no theory, all that really matters is how much we like a particular composition. And music theory will allow you to have an even deeper understanding of the music you like, just as color theory reveals the physics of painting, and linguistics explains the grammar of poetry.

QUO VADIS?

Before someone sets out on the journey to learn music theory, there's a misconception that at some point you'll be "finished." Is that the way you feel now? I'll bet that you may be more interested in continuing than looking back at what you have learned. If you have worked through every section of this book, you are now able to speak the common language of music theory. As it was hinted to in the Prélude, all of the questions that this book may have answered for you have probably been replaced by an entirely new set. This will go on and on, and it's what makes music endlessly intriguing. Now that you have a formidable set of musical tools, there's no theoretical concept that can elude your discovery, no musical discussion where you'll feel left out, no written music that will appear as nonsense, and no limitation that can hold you back. Welcome to the world of musicians…

GLOSSARY OF TERMS

accidental: A symbol placed adjacent to a note that raises or lowers the pitch chromatically: natural, flat, sharp, double sharp, and double flat.

amplitude: The relative difference in density between an adjacent crest and trough in a sound wave; also referred to as *volume*.

aperiodic: A wave whose succession of crests and troughs does not repeat or form a pattern; also referred to as *noise*.

asymmetric meter: A meter whose beat groupings are uneven.

bar: *See measure.*

bar line: A vertical line through a staff that indicates the end of a measure.

beat: The basic unit of meter in music.

chord: A collection of three or more discrete pitches.

chromatic: Pitches that do not belong to a prevailing key.

circle of fifths: The organization of key signatures arranged by increments of one accidental. Beginning with C, the tonic of each sharp key can be found by ascending a fifth above the previous tonic, and the tonic of each flat key can be found by descending a fifth below the previous tonic.

clef: A symbol placed at the beginning of a staff to indicate its pitch range.

compound interval: A dyad whose size is greater than one octave.

crest: The highest point of amplitude found in a sound wave.

diatonic: A collection of pitches that belong to a prevailing key. Also called the *diatonic collection*.

dyad: A collection of two separate pitches. *See interval.*

enharmonic: Having the same sound but a different name (e.g., A♭ and G♯).

equalization (e.q.): Manipulation of specific frequency bands found in a sound wave.

frequency: The number of periodic crests occurring per second in a sound wave, measured in Hertz (Hz).

fundamental: The lowest pitch of the overtone series.

harmonics: The pitches of the overtone series found above the fundamental.

hemiola: When beats grouped in three are re-grouped in two (and vice-versa), temporarily changing the beat of the prevailing meter.

hertz (Hz): A unit of measurement expressed as cycles per second, indicating the frequency of a sound wave.

interval: A collection of two separate pitches, described in terms of size and quality.

inversion: When the lowest-sounding pitch is any chord member other than its root.

key: In Western tonal music, a collection of seven discrete pitches with one pitch identified as the tonic, which in turn generates a hierarchy of influence on the remaining pitches; the pitches are organized in a specific pattern of half and whole steps.

leap: Any melodic intervallic distance larger than a whole step.

ledger line: A short line to accommodate a note that needs to be written above or below a five-line staff.

legato: A direction to play a musical passage in a smooth and connected manner.

loco: Italian for "at place," often used to cancel an *ottava* sign.

measure: The basic unit of meter, which is indicated by bar lines on the staff; also called a *bar*.

meter: The regular grouping of beats.

mode: Scale constructions similar to the major and minor scale, but with a chromatically-altered tone or tones.

octave: The intervallic distance of eight consecutive steps through the musical alphabet.

ottava: A symbol—either *8va* or *8vb*—indicating which notes should be played either an octave higher or lower than written, respectively.

overtone series: The collection of audible pitches generated by a vibrating object, such as a string.

periodic: Regular and predictable; a pattern.

pitch: The basic tone-unit of music, represented by one of the first seven letters of the alphabet.

polymeter: Two or more simultaneously-occurring meters whereby the beat is shared but the beat groupings differ.

polyrhythm: Two or more simultaneously-occurring rhythms—often *within* a measure—that do not share a common beat grouping or division, but evenly divide the same amount of time (e.g., 4 equal beats in the same space as 5 equal beats). Polyrhythms that occur *across* measures can sometimes be described in terms of *polymeter*.

position: A description of a chord determined by the lowest-sounding note.

quality: A means of sub-classifying intervals (and chords) that share the same category of size (e.g., thirds). The five qualities are: major, minor, diminished, augmented, and perfect.

rest: A symbol for a specific duration of silence.

scale: A collection of pitches, usually within an octave, arranged in a specific order of half and whole steps.

scale degree: The numeric position a pitch occupies in a scale.

slash chords: A symbol that indicates the chord name (on the left side of the slash) and what should be the lowest-sounding note (on the right side of the slash). For example: Amaj7/C♯.

slur: A curved line drawn over or under a collection of notes, indicating they should be played legato.

staccato: An accent that indicates a note should be performed detached and separated.

staff: Five lines written horizontally upon which music is traditionally written.

step: The smallest intervallic distance (in Western tonal music) that involves two discrete pitches is a *half* step. The distance of two half steps is considered a *whole* step. Any intervallic distance larger than a whole step is considered a *leap*.

syncopation: When the weak part of the beat receives emphasis.

tempo: The relative rate at which the beat occurs through time.

tie: A curved line connecting noteheads on the same pitch, indicating they should be performed as one note.

timbre: Any tone-characteristic of a pitch other than its frequency (e.g., an upright bass has a "darker timbre" than an electric bass).

triad: A collection of three discrete pitches in successive thirds; also called a *chord*.

trough: The lowest point of amplitude found in a sound wave.